CANNING &
PRESERVING YOUR
OWN HARVEST

AN ENCYCLOPEDIA OF COUNTRY LIVING GUIDE

CANNING & PRESERVING YOUR OWN HARVEST

Carla Emery & Lorene Edwards Forkner

SASQUATCH BOOKS
SEATTLE

Portions of this book have appeared, in the same words or in substance, in *The Encyclopedia of Country Living*, 10th edition (Sasquatch Books, 2008).

Printed in the United States of America
Published by Sasquatch Books
Distributed by PGW/Perseus
15 14 13 12 11 10 09   9 8 7 6 5 4 3 2 1

Cover illustrations: Kate Quinby and
    Clipart.com/2009© Jupiterimages Corporation
Cover design: Rosebud Eustace; based on *The Encyclopedia of Country Living, 10th Edition* cover
    design by Kate Basart/Union Pageworks
Interior design and composition: Jennifer Shontz, Red Shoe Design
Interior illustrations: Kate Quinby and
    Clipart.com/2009© Jupiterimages Corporation

Library of Congress Cataloging-in-Publication Data
Emery, Carla.
  Canning and preserving your own harvest : an encyclopedia of country living guide / Carla Emery
& Lorene Edwards Forkner.
      p. cm.
  Includes bibliographical references and index.
  ISBN-13: 978-1-57061-571-9
  ISBN-10: 1-57061-571-3
  1. Canning and preserving. I. Forkner, Lorene Edwards. II. Title.
  TX601.E64 2009
  641.4—dc22

                  2009018164

Sasquatch Books
119 South Main Street, Suite 400
Seattle, WA 98104
(206) 467-4300
www.sasquatchbooks.com
custserv@sasquatchbooks.com

For all of us with fond memories of hot summer days picking
blackberries, sticky kitchen counters, and glorious jam—
why is it so hard to get kids to pick berries these days?

—LEF

CONTENTS

INTRODUCTION

Today preserving is enjoying renewed popularity and extending the harvest is once again hip. Practices that began generations ago as sensible household economies have more recently become emblematic of resolute independence. At the middle of the twentieth century, many believed our country to be poised on the brink of nuclear war; fear was systemic and the world was a frightening place. The back-to-the-land movement, largely composed of disillusioned young adults, sought to withdraw from city life, with its many advances and perceived failed political systems, to seek a more self-sufficient lifestyle in an effort to survive the feared coming apocalypse. Naïve? Perhaps. Resourceful? Most certainly. It was with this motivation that Carla Emery, her family, and many others like them moved to the country, where they began to rediscover the once-routine life skills of their grandparents' and great-grandparents' generations. Carla began keeping a record of these nearly lost country arts and practices, coupled with her passionate, concerned, and astute observations, chronicling her trials and victories alike. Today, thirty-five years after she first began the adventure, *The Encyclopedia of Country Living*, now in its tenth edition, remains a living history and comprehensive resource for "living off the land and doing it yourself."

These days, growing concerns about food safety and security routinely generate frightening headlines, and an unstable economy has us all thinking about cost-cutting measures. However, even in the midst of contemporary crises and economic anxiety, for many of us the delicious pleasures of the table are never far from our thoughts and menus. This book is less about surviving calamity or amassing a collection of dusty jars and piles of mystery packages at the back of the freezer than it is about making the most of fresh, seasonal bounty, putting up healthy foods, and producing delicious treats for a well-stocked pantry, meant to be shared with friends and family.

When important principles are followed, traditional preserving methods—freezing, canning, drying, and live storage—do a fine job of keeping provisions. Beyond these basics, vinegar, sugar, alcohol, and other cures are primarily employed for the additional flavor they impart as well as their effectiveness at prolonging the shelf life of various foodstuffs. Through their almost magical alchemy, food is not just preserved but transformed and elevated into something altogether different to become the fare of festive celebrations and artisan craftsmanship. Before we get into the complexities of water baths, microbes, temperature controls, and enzyme activity, I leave you with these simple instructions: savor the season—harvest, preserve, share—and enjoy. Repeat.

—Lorene Edwards Forkner
August 2009

PART ONE

STORING YOUR BOUNTY

HISTORICAL PERSPECTIVE AND OUR CHANGING MOTIVATION

Everything old is new again. We are in the midst of a contemporary revival of almost-lost kitchen arts coupled with a newfound respect for food integrity and healthful living. In a welcome departure from our recent history of fast, global, and often anonymous food, America is developing a palate and a passion for fresh, seasonal fare as well as a growing respect for the farmers and artisan craftspeople who work so hard to produce it.

Until fairly recently (certainly within the past couple of generations) families harvested crops in the fall and stored enough food to get them through until the next harvest. They were frugal by necessity; nothing was allowed to go to waste. A routine part of housekeeping involved mastering a battery of various preserving skills that customarily were passed from generation to generation along with grandmother's china, family stories, and a tendency toward red hair or blue eyes.

Prior to World War II, all food was organic and most likely raised or produced in the general vicinity of where it was consumed. The post-war boom economy saw a population shift toward urban life, along with the rise of commercial farming and larger, more complicated distribution systems. Factory and office workers became dependent on grocery stores that in turn relied on truck routes and the railway, shuffling food from field to processing plant to store shelves. Food security, which had once been quite literally in house, was now outsourced to the factory farm.

There was a time when milk, butter, and cheese from dairy animals, along with meat and stored food, were the backbone of a winter diet, and fresh greens and tree- or vine-ripened fruit were enjoyed and celebrated for the ephemeral seasonal pleasures they brought to the table. The seasons dictated the menu, and one's preserving skills meant the difference between a bounteous menu and lean times. In Carla's words, "If people's labors were fruitful, they put away a long-term food supply as a matter of common sense; their food was wholesome, hearty, and healthy."

These days we have strawberries in December, oranges throughout the year, and goods from around the world shipped to the shelves of even the smallest corner grocery store. We have access to a diet rich in variety and seemingly independent of geographic or seasonal boundaries. However, preservatives and other additives that lengthen shelf life and allow foods to withstand the rigors of world travel are being held responsible for more and more health issues, and a quickly expanding national waistline proves that more is not always better.

Petroleum-based fertilizers, herbicides, and pesticides—once thought to be a farmer's best friend and the "modern" answer to feeding large populations—render us heavily reliant on foreign oil and vulnerable to rising fuel costs. With food costs soaring, we've clocked the miles represented by the meal on our plate, only to find ourselves helplessly dependent on a food web completely outside our control.

A new face of environmental concern has emerged that focuses on supporting local producers of naturally delicious and organic food, produced sustainably, under fair and just working conditions. City and suburban residents alike are trading in their lawns for productive vegetable gardens, community vegetable gardens are spreading like clover, and we're discovering flavor and variety alongside satisfaction and sufficiency. Farmers markets and community supported agriculture (CSA) shares provide us with farm fresh goods whether we have a plot of land or not.

The advance of wireless technology has allowed more businesses (and their families) to relocate to small towns and rural areas in pursuit of a more affordable cost of living, a slower pace, and a sense of community sometimes difficult to attain in a big city environment. Many of these new households come complete with vegetable gardens and possibly even orchards, putting fresh food right in their own backyard. Second homes in the country with generous landholdings are supporting weekend farmers and ambitious recreational cooks.

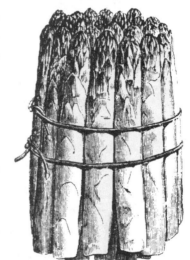

More and more of us are digging in to discover regional foods and farmers markets, eagerly anticipating the shifting bounty at local u-pick stands. We're learning a new calendar of seasonal crops and planning our meals—and gardens—to reflect this awareness. There is a heartfelt satisfaction in the kitchen of a gardening household when homegrown food becomes a delicious meal on the table. Not only are you producing clean, healthy food free of preservatives and toxins, but the savings in your food budget can be generous, and you're receiving maximum value in nutrition and health. And the flavors—oh my!

SEASONAL EATING

The first rule of seasonal eating is to enjoy that which cannot be preserved in its natural state—crisp green salads; fresh vine-ripened tomatoes still warm from the summer sun; richly perfumed fragile berries; luscious, juicy stone fruit; and the pungent aroma of flavorful fresh herbs. When summer corn is ripe and abundant, we have it every day, simply steamed or roasted, dripping with butter, and seasoned with pure salt and pepper. These seasonal flavors and dining experiences are gifts of the present, best enjoyed simply and appreciated in their prime. Once the season ends and we've gnawed the last cob of corn and wiped the sticky fruit juices from our chin, then we really begin to value our stores of preserved food.

Next, learn those foods that are easy to keep or hold in a ripened state. With little or no work on your part, apart from creating and monitoring proper storage conditions, potatoes, winter squash and pumpkins, onions, garlic, and some tree fruit can become the foundation of fresh meals throughout the year.

We've all found the errant dusty jar at the back of the cupboard dating from the Reagan administration; when assembling a larder of preserved foods, plan for appropriate quantities, not the End Times. In an effort to preserve energy—yours and the utility company's—process only what you can eat or give away before the next harvest. In addition to freeing up storage space, you'll also enjoy your preserves while they're at their best.

Preserving methods may enable food to be held for stable, long-term storage or involve quicker projects for more immediate satisfaction. Freeze a bumper crop of strawberries now for jamming or processing once the heat of the summer has abated, or put up a quick pickle of carrots, beans, or cucumbers to spice up summer picnics and barbecues right now.

Finally, keep track of your efforts in a seasonal preserving notebook; this can help you plan for the future, monitor your inventory, and record favorite recipes. Notes to yourself at the completion of each project can suggest improvements or variations, as well as help you avoid repeating the same mistake twice. Whether it's as simple as an actual notebook or card file or as sophisticated as even a rudimentary computer database, any information you record will help you to maximize your resources.

You might choose to organize your notebook by season to remind yourself to freeze rhubarb in spring, order strawberries from Boy Scouts in June, and pick beans for pickling in the summer. Are you curious to try homemade brandied fruit and happen to have neighbors with a productive plum tree? Make a note to yourself to approach them about the notion of pooling your efforts; plum picking in exchange for brandied plums is not a bad trade. A reminder to place your order early in the season for an organically raised hog, side of beef, or heirloom turkey will help the farmer who needs to plan for his coming "crop" and ensures that you won't miss out when quantities are limited.

Make notes about previous shortages and special preferences. Did your family despair when the blackberry jam ran out? A friendly reminder in August and September when berries are ripe might just send them out picking so you can put aside even more jars for the coming winter.

SAMPLE PRESERVING NOTES

Notes Template:

Season:	
Crop (variety):	
Source:	
Process (recipe):	
Seasonal notes:	

Examples:

Season:	Summer
Crop (variety):	Peaches (Pence Orchard in Eastern Washington!!)
Source:	Farmers market, grocery store
Process (recipe):	Freeze, jam, infused liquor (see page 88)
Seasonal notes:	Available only when *tree-ripened* in August and early September, depending on the weather. Very short shelf life.

Season:	Early spring
Crop (variety):	Nettles
Source:	Next door weed lot
Process (recipe):	Blanch and freeze in zip-locking bags (see page 18)
Seasonal notes:	Pick (with gloves!) only the top 4 to 6 inches of the emerging plants, which are the most tender.

Season:	Late summer
Crop (variety):	Wild blackberries
Source:	Neighborhood greenbelt
Process (recipe):	Jam or jelly and syrup
Seasonal notes:	Force the kids to help pick!

Season:	Any time
Crop (variety):	Fresh carrots, beans, radishes, shallots
Source:	Home garden, farmers market, grocery
Process (recipe):	Quick pickle (see page 106)
Seasonal notes:	Takes only a day or less. Great with barbecue!

PRESERVING

O ur environment is rife with life forms that compete for nourishment. Molds, yeasts, and bacteria—invisible though they may be—are ever-present in the air we breathe, water we drink, surfaces in our home, the soil—even our food. Time doesn't spoil food; food rots or goes bad when the natural enzymes responsible for ripening and microorganisms present in our environment go unchecked. "Preserving" is simply an effort to slow or delay these processes to extend the shelf life of food. All stored foods, no matter how they are preserved, will slowly but steadily lose quality and nutritional value, and in time spoil, as home preserving methods can never completely eliminate the various risk factors.

PRESERVING FUNDAMENTALS

The best-tasting and most healthful preserves are a careful marriage of these elements:

▶ Proper selection and harvest methods, using the highest-quality raw materials

▶ Correct handling and technique, matching the appropriate method of preservation to the intended crop and meticulously adhering to safety measures (see chart, page 179)

▶ Appropriate storage practices

In this book we'll examine the four primary methods of preserving food: freezing, canning, drying, and "live" storage (what our great-grandparents called a root cellar). Freezing food suspends or dramatically slows the process of decay. Canning, when done correctly, kills organisms with heat and creates a sealed environment to keep other spoilers out. Drying removes moisture that enzymes and microorganisms need to reproduce. Live storage takes advantage of certain living foods' natural defenses against spoilage.

From there, we'll look at how food is preserved and transformed through the addition of various cures—vinegar, sugar, alcohol, salt, fat, and smoke. A cucumber is simply a refreshing salad in summer, but tangy pickles are a time-honored side at many holiday celebrations; fresh peaches may be a fleeting summer pleasure, but doused in alcohol, they become a jewel-colored treasure and a glimpse back to the warmth of summer on a cold winter's evening.

The recipes for fruits, vegetables, and herbs encompass jams, jellies, pickles, condiments and sauces both savory and sweet, cordials, syrups, herbal infusions, and flavorful tea and spice blends. We'll also explore other preserving arts nearly lost to the home kitchen in this day of quick, processed, factory food. Access to farmers markets and a growing demand for organic meat on grocery shelves means today we can purchase fresh, healthy meat—raised and butchered responsibly—in economical large cuts to portion up and freeze. Plus, old-world curing methods, coupled with today's science, allow us to explore artisan methods of charcuterie, resulting in a superior finished homemade product free of hormones and antibiotics. Organic dairies offer milk, cream, yogurt, goldenrod-yolked fresh eggs, and tangy cheeses as grassy as the grazing pastures that went into them. Homemade cheese is quick, flavorful, and fresh in flavor compared to store-bought versions filled with gums and stabilizers. The process is easy—the result so satisfying.

Home preserving may not be for everyone. Busy lives, demanding careers, and precious little leisure time dictate our limits. But generally speaking, those who pursue these somewhat old-school arts are generous—not just with their efforts, but also in sharing their table and resources with those who cannot or have not. We're on a culinary adventure as we learn the resourceful ways of generations that came before us. It's a path of economic thrift and simple luxuries, rich in flavor and tradition, executed in concert with the seasons and with respect for our environment.

FREEZING

No doubt due to its ease and the speed with which quantities of food can be processed, freezing is the most popular method for home preserving. Freezing retains more nutrients than any other form of food preservation, and it is very safe. However, for serious food storage you'll need a separate upright or chest-type freezer capable of maintaining temperatures well below freezing, ideally at −5°F. Equip yourself with a reliable thermometer; the freezer life of food drops dramatically at even a few degrees above zero. Even at low temperatures, frozen food will deteriorate and spoil over time due to cryophilic (cold-loving) microbes. Only temperatures of 0°F and lower keep these organisms inactive; anything warmer, even for a short while, introduces the risk of spoilage.

A freezer is completely dependent on a reliable energy source for power. Fuel costs being what they are these days, it makes sense to organize, pack, and maintain your freezer for optimum efficiency. A freezer that is 70 to 80 percent full requires less energy to keep cold and will hold its temperature for longer in the event of a power outage. Cardboard milk cartons filled with water and frozen will suffice to fill empty space until your shelves are sufficiently filled with food. Maintain a good seal on the door and keep openings to a quick minimum.

The bigger your freezer is, the more food it can handle freezing at once. However, the more unfrozen food you put into a freezer at one time, the longer it will take the appliance to freeze it. Refer to the manufacturer's manual that came with the freezer for guidelines as to the maximum amount that can be frozen at one time. A general rule of thumb is to add no more than 2 to 3 pounds of food per cubic foot of freezer space. For example, a 16-cubic-foot freezer should not have more than 35 pounds of unfrozen food put into it in one 24-hour period.

As your frozen food stores accumulate, it's a good idea to keep an inventory taped to the outside of your freezer. Record what you froze in each package of food and when, crossing off each item as you remove it.

IMPORTANT FACTORS FOR FREEZING SUCCESS

Quality: Start with high-quality, fresh food. Young, tender fruits and vegetables processed quickly after harvest ensure the best results.

Prepare and pre-treat: Clean food thoroughly, scrubbing with a medium-stiff bristled brush as necessary in a sink filled with cold water. Lift the food out of the water to leave behind grit that has settled to the bottom of the sink. Slice vegetables or fruit and pretreat to preserve the best color and texture over time. (See chart, page 19.)

Package: Package food in appropriate serving portions and in such a way as to remove as much air as possible; seal securely. "Freezer burn" occurs when a container isn't completely sealed; air gets in to oxidize and dehydrate the food, making it appear faded and dried out. Be sure to clearly label the package with its contents and freezing date (see example, opposite).

Contents:	Fava beans	2009					
Jan	July	1	2	3	4	5	6
Feb	Aug	7	(8)	9	10	11	12
Mar	Sept	13	14	15	16	17	18
Apr	Oct	19	20	21	22	23	24
May	Nov	25	26	27	28	29	30
(June)	Dec	31					

(Leftmost vertical label: **Frozen on:**)

Freeze quickly: Twenty-four hours before you're going to be doing a major freezing project, turn your freezer temperature to −10°F. Quick freezing minimizes the risk of spoilage and reduces ice-crystal formation, which in turn minimizes mushiness. Place packages of unfrozen food in the coldest part of the freezer. For even faster processing, spread food out in a single layer on a sheet pan and place in the freezer; when frozen, package or bag it for long-term storage. Once all the packaged food has been frozen, organize the freezer for long-term storage and turn the temperature back to 0°F.

PACKAGING

Plastic Freezer Containers—Made of food-grade, rigid plastic with airtight covers that seal securely, these are easy to label and stack without difficulty to fill space efficiently.

Jars—Choose wide mouth freezer jars with straight sides. Leave ½ inch headspace at the top for pints, 1 inch for quarts; to allow for expansion of the jar's contents when frozen.

Bags—Nonrigid, food safe, zip-locking freezer bags or home-sealed boilable bags allow you to package and fill the freezer with the least waste of space, as the bags conform to the containers around them.

Freezer Wraps—Butcher paper (sometimes referred to as *laminated paper* or *locker paper*), plastic wrap, or heavy duty *freezer-grade* foil can all be used to securely wrap solid foods. When using a wrap, press it around the food to eliminate as much air as possible, and secure with freezer tape to ensure a moisture- and vapor-proof package.

FREEZER STORAGE TIMES FOR BEST QUALITY

It is best to use all frozen foods within one year. These storage times indicate the period in which food retains its best quality.

Fish and Meat

Fish	2 to 3 months
Meat and poultry, raw	8 to 12 months
Meat, ground	2 to 3 months
Cured meat	1 to 2 months

Dairy and Eggs

Butter	6 to 9 months
Eggs (whole, whites, yolks)	12 months
Milk	1 month
Yogurt (plain)	1 month

Fruits

Fruit and fruit juice (not citrus)	12 months
Citrus fruit and juice	4 to 6 months

Vegetables

Vegetables, uncooked (except onions)	12 months
Onions, uncooked	3 to 6 months
Herbs	4 to 6 months

Other Foods

Jams and jellies	9 to 12 months
Fruit sauces and butters	6 months

VEGETABLES

Most vegetables benefit from a blanching pretreatment if they are to be frozen for longer than three months. The heat of blanching puts a halt to ripening enzymes, thereby preserving color, texture, and nutrients. Food may be blanched with boiling water or hot steam, which preserves the freshest flavor and a greater number of vitamins.

▶ *Steam blanch:* Put a steamer basket or a colander that will fit into a deep, covered pot filled with 2 to 3 inches of boiling water. Place sliced vegetables in a thin layer in the basket and cover. Begin to time blanching when you see steam emerging from the pot.

▶ *Boiling blanch:* Bring to boil 1 gallon of water for every 1 pound of vegetables. Immerse the prepared vegetables in hot water, stirring briefly to ensure even heat distribution. Cover and begin timing from the moment the water returns to a boil.

Immediately after blanching, remove the vegetables from the steam or hot water and plunge them into an ice water bath to cool them as quickly as possible. Thoroughly drain and pack for freezing.

PRETREATING VEGETABLES FOR FREEZING			
	Preparation	Steam blanch (in minutes)*	Boiling blanch (in minutes)*
Artichoke	Small, trimmed	8–10	8
Asparagus	Medium spears	4	3
Beans, snap	Young, tender	3	2
Beans, shell	Green	1–2	n/a
Broccoli	Cut into florets, pare stems	3–6	2–4
Brussels sprouts	Uniform size	3–6	2–4
Cauliflower	Cut into florets, pare stems	5	3
Corn, cut from cob	Remove husks and silk; blanch, cool, and cut from cob	6	4
Eggplant	Small, tender, sliced; acid dip to preserve color	4–6	2–4
Greens (beet, cabbage, chard, collards, kale, spinach)		2–3	n/a
Okra	Young, whole pods	2–3	3–4
Peas, shelling	Remove pods	3	2
Peas, snow/snap	Whole	3	2
Peppers, sweet	Roast, skin, and pack	n/a	n/a
Pumpkin and winter squash	Bake or boil until tender, purée and pack	n/a	Varies by size
Squash, summer	Sliced	3	3
Vegetables, mixed	Blanch separately and combine after chilling	Consult individual vegetable instructions	Consult individual vegetable instructions

*Add 1 minute to blanching time if you live 5,000 feet or more above sea level.

FRUIT

Fruit may be simply sliced or crushed and packed in containers with water or juice for freezing; it is not absolutely necessary to pretreat fruit. Berries and sliced fruit may be quick frozen on sheet pans as described earlier and dry-packed loose in bags or containers. However, fruit that has been packed in sugar or sweetened syrup will hold its shape and texture better during longer storage, and an antioxidant treatment will prevent light-colored fruit from darkening over time.

ANTIOXIDANT TREATMENT

To prevent discoloration of light-colored fruits and the other deteriorating effects of oxidation, briefly dip prepared fruit into one of the following solutions:

Dip	Suggested for	Ingredients	Time
Ascorbic Acid	All fruits	2 tablespoons ascorbic acid or five 1-gram vitamin C tablets, crushed, dissolved in 1 quart water	Dip for 5 minutes
Honey	Bananas, peaches, pineapple	3 cups water, 1 cup sugar—heat, then stir in 1 cup honey	Dip and remove immediately
Juice	Apples, bananas, peaches	1 quart pineapple juice, 1 quart warm water, 1/4 cup lemon juice	Dip for 5 to 10 minutes
Pectin	Berries, cherries, peaches	1 box powdered pectin, 1 cup water; boil for 1 minute, add 1/2 cup sugar and enough cold water to make 2 cups	Glaze fruit with thin coating
Salt	All fruits	6 tablespoons pickling salt in 1 gallon water	Dip for 5 minutes

SUGAR AND SYRUP PACKS

Mix ½ cup granulated sugar with every pound of fruit and stir until the sugar dissolves. Pack into containers and freeze. To pack fruit in a sugar syrup, add ½ cup cold sugar syrup of your choice (see the following chart) to a 2-cup container packed with prepared fruit and freeze.

Thin	2 cups sugar*	4 cups water	5 cups finished syrup
Medium	3 cups sugar*	4 cups water	5½ cups finished syrup
Heavy	8 cups sugar	4 cups water	8 cups finished syrup

*Honey may be substituted for sugar for a thin syrup (1 cup honey/3 cups water) or medium syrup (1 cup honey/2 cups water). Completely immerse sliced fruit in the honey syrup, pack into containers, and freeze. Honey has inherent preservative qualities that prevent fruit from darkening, eliminating the need for an acid dip.

MEAT

With virtually no effect on flavor or texture, freezing is the best way to preserve and hold meat for long-term storage. Most farmers markets now have at least one purveyor of fresh meat at some point during the year, and many small family farms offer large economical cuts of meat raised free of antibiotics, hormones, and questionable husbandry practices, offering both health and financial rewards.

Divide your cuts of meat into appropriate serving portions and securely wrap, using a double layer of moisture-proof, heavily waxed freezer paper. Ground meat can be stored in rolls, blocks, or ready-to-cook patties. Label the package with the kind of meat, the cut, and the date it was frozen. Quickly freeze and store at 0°F.

If you are expecting to process an amount of meat that exceeds the capacity of your appliance to safely freeze in one batch, you may want to work with the butcher to prefreeze the meat for you or purchase space in a commercial freezer storage locker, transferring smaller amounts to your home freezer as needed. *Note: If you want to store meat in your freezer for a long time, keep in mind that unsalted, unseasoned, unground meat keeps the longest.*

FISH AND SHELLFISH

Freeze fish and shellfish immediately after you catch or buy it. Raw seafood may contain harmful microorganisms and must be properly handled to avoid food poisoning. Carefully wash your hands, utensils, and all work surfaces after handling raw seafood, and never let it come into contact with cooked seafood. Keep fish and shellfish covered, moist, and cold—on ice or in the refrigerator. Handle carefully to prevent crushing and bruising, which invites spoilage.

Clean fish in fresh cold water, cut into fillets or steaks, and divide into appropriate serving portions. Small fish weighing 2 pounds or less may be gutted and frozen whole. A 30-second dip in a 5-percent salt solution (^{2}⁄$_3$ cup salt in 1 gallon water) before wrapping and freezing will improve keeping quality.

To freeze lobster and crab, cook them without salt, remove meat from the shell, pack into clean containers, and freeze. Shrimp are best frozen raw, as they toughen when cooked and then frozen. Clams, oysters, and scallops should be shelled and packed raw, in their liquor or a brine made from 1 tablespoon salt dissolved in 3 cups of water.

HERBS

Choose herbs at the peak of their season when they have the maximum amount of flavorful oils, and process quickly to preserve their fresh taste. Before freezing, briefly blanch bundles of herbs to preserve their bright color. Hold small bundles of herbs with tongs and immerse in boiling water for no more than a few seconds. Drain and cool on towels before packaging in freezer bags. Even easier, chop fresh herbs finely and place them in a clean ice cube tray; each compartment will hold a couple of tablespoons of the chopped herb, a good portion size. Add boiling water to cover the herbs in the trays and freeze. There's no need for additional blanching. Once the cubes are solid, pop them out of the tray and package in a freezer bag or container; label and date. These herb cubes can be added directly to sauces, stews and other preparations without thawing.

Best herbs for freezing: basil, chives, chervil, cilantro, dill leaves, lovage, mint, savory, and tarragon.

CANNING

Heat is the weapon the home canner wields in the battle against decay and toxins. Thermophiles—bacteria that thrive at relatively high temperatures that would kill most other microorganisms—are of special concern for canners. Improper canning procedures can be deadly. It is very important to work with contemporary recipes that take into account the latest technology and

science. Follow instructions carefully—this is not the time for experimentation, as consequences could prove lethal. Never does it count more to play things safe and by the rules than when you are canning.

IMPORTANT FACTORS FOR CANNING SUCCESS

Clean Food: The more microorganisms in food to start with, the more heat treatment is needed to eliminate them. Start with fresh, unspoiled food free from bruises or spots of decay and wash thoroughly in clean water.

   Acidity: Different foods naturally contain varying amounts of acid, which works to control microbial activity. Acid level is measured by the pH scale, which runs from 1 to 14: 7 is neutral, neither alkaline nor acid; numbers lower than 7 indicate greater acidity levels. (See chart, opposite.)

   Canning Temperature: High-acid foods can be processed more quickly and at slightly lower temperatures—that is, the boiling point or 212°F—than low-acid foods. To be safe, low-acid foods must be processed at 240°F; you must use a pressure canner to get sustained temperatures that high.

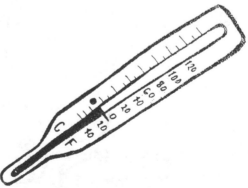

Processing Time: The higher the temperature, the shorter the time needed to kill dangerous microorganisms. Whether you *hot pack* or *raw pack* affects processing time; packing instruction and processing times are indicated in canning recipes. Hot packing involves filling jars with hot, precooked food. When raw packing—preserving food that is jarred at room temperature or colder—the food must be processed for longer periods.

Pack Density: When processing, heat travels from the outer surface of the jar inward toward the center. Large jars and food with an especially dense texture, such as solid-pack squash, require longer heat processing to ensure that the appropriate temperature, necessary to kill dangerous bacteria, is reached throughout the contents. Loosely packed food bathed in liquid heats much more quickly and efficiently.

THE PH OF COMMON FOODS		
212°F Water bath	1	n/a
	2	Plums, pickles
	3	Gooseberries, sour cherries, apricots, apples, blackberries, peaches
	4	Sauerkraut, sweet cherries, pears, tomatoes*
240°F Pressure can	5	Okra, pumpkin, carrots, turnips, cabbage, beets, snap beans, spinach, asparagus, cauliflower
	6	Lima beans, corn, peas
	7	n/a

*Researchers have determined that the acid content of tomatoes at harvest is dependent on variety, degree of ripeness, and the conditions under which they were grown.

ABOUT BOTULISM

Clostridium botulinum is a bacterium prevalent in most soils. The mature bacteria are not poisonous, but in spore form it is a naturally occurring, poisonous nerve toxin responsible for botulism, a rare but deadly illness. Approximately one hundred botulism cases are reported each year in the United States. Most of these involve infants whose not-yet-fully-developed intestinal tract is less resistant to the bacteria in any form; for this reason it is recommended that children under the age of one not play in garden soil. The small number of reported cases of food-borne botulism can generally be traced to home-canned foods.

Foods with a high sugar or acid content are naturally inhospitable to this deadly spore, which is why fruit, pickles, and jams may be processed at lower water-bath temperatures. However, in the absence of sugar and acid, heat is the only remaining defense. If unchecked by heat, the spores replicate and give off an invisible, tasteless, but powerful toxin. Heat-resistant botulism spores are reliably killed at 240°F—a temperature achieved only by heating under pressure—"pressure canning." Botulism-contaminated food does not look or smell "off" yet this poisoning is usually fatal—an unnecessary risk you can avoid by assiduously following proper canning instructions and rules. Better safe than sorry: when in doubt, throw it out!

Equipment and supplies

Jars—To minimize spoilage, select jars based on what you are canning and how quickly it will be consumed. Canning jars are available in ½ pint, pint, and quart sizes. Wide mouth jars have an opening the same as their diameter, making them easy to fill and thoroughly clean. Jams, jellies, and specialty condiments are generally processed in ½ pint or pint jars; pickles, vegetables, and fruits fit best in larger jars. *Note: Do not use antique canning jars—neither the zinc-lidded jars nor the old two-piece glass-lidded type—because their seals are not dependable. New decorative and "European" style jars are available in specialty kitchen stores and make a nice presentation for gifts.*

   Lids—Common two-piece lids consist of a *single-use* lid and a matching screw band; make sure you purchase the right size lids and screw bands to match your jars. The screw bands, like jars and unlike lids, can be used over and over until they rust or get bent, either of which can hinder a complete seal.

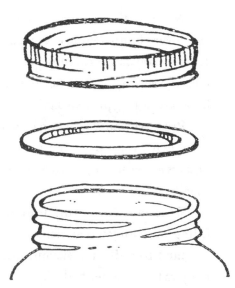

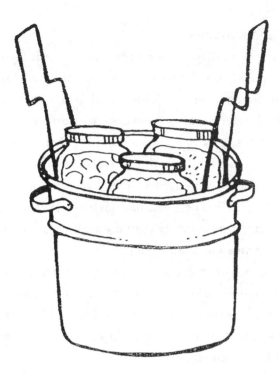

Water-bath canning kettle—Any container large enough to hold jars covered with boiling water can serve as a water-bath canning kettle. Traditional enamel canning kettles come equipped with a jar-holding rack to keep jars off the bottom of the pan; this prevents jostling and breakage during processing.

Pressure canner—A somewhat expensive but one-time cost, and absolutely necessary if you plan to can low-acid foods. *Note: Pressure canners are potentially dangerous. Make sure you have a manual and follow its instructions to the letter.*

Wide mouth canning funnel—Facilitates handling hot food and filling jars with fewer spills.

Jar lifter—Heat-resistant, pincer-like tongs for safely removing hot jars from a water bath.

Lid lifter—A plastic wand with a magnet at one end for lifting metal lids out of hot water.

The following common kitchen utensils will ease processing and protect you from the heat involved:

- Hot pads, mitts, heavy potholders
- Jar/bottle brush
- Kitchen timer
- Ladle
- Slotted spoon
- Tongs

GENERAL INSTRUCTIONS

Preparing and packing

1. Before you begin, inspect jar rims for cracks and nicks, which can prevent a proper seal.

2. Meticulously clean jars, lids, and screw bands in hot soapy water and rinse thoroughly. Keep jars and lids hot in scalding water until ready to fill. Although a dishwasher is not a must, it is a real timesaver, as it can wash large batches of jars and lids and hold them at the proper temperature until needed. *Note: To avoid possible shattering, never pour boiling water or hot food into a cool jar, and never place a cool jar directly into boiling water.*

3. Fill hot jars with the prepared recipe, carefully following directions for either hot pack or raw pack procedures. Work quickly to ensure the jars do not cool, or they may crack when they contact the boiling water.

4. When packing jars, allow the proper headspace indicated in the recipe to accommodate expansion of food during processing. Too little headspace can force food past the lid and prevent a sound seal.

5. After filling, release any air bubbles trapped in the jar by running a kitchen knife or other thin, flat utensil around the inner walls of the jar.

6. Wipe the rims with a clean damp cloth before placing the heated lid on the jar, with the "composition" side next to the glass. Secure the lid with a screw band.

7. Proceed according to the processing method.

Water-bath canning procedure

1. Load the jars into the jar rack and, using the two handles, carefully lower it into the boiling water in the canning kettle. Adjust the water level so that it is at least 1 inch above the tops of the jars. Cover the canner with its lid.

2. Start timing when the water returns to a full boil and process for the length of time indicated in your recipe. Do not allow the water to fall beneath the appropriate level or drop below a boil.

ALTITUDE ADJUSTMENTS FOR WATER-BATH CANNING

At sea level water boils at 212°F. With increasing altitude, water will boil at lower temperatures, which are less efficient to sufficiently kill dangerous bacteria. Therefore, for canning safety you must increase your processing time based on your altitude. Most recipes are written for processing from sea level to 1,000 feet.

Altitude	Processing Time
Under 1,000 feet	As stated in recipe
1,000 to 3,000 feet	Time stated plus 5 minutes
3,000 to 6,000 feet	Time stated plus 10 minutes
Above 6,000 feet	Time stated plus 15 minutes

Pressure canning procedure

Pressure canning is the only safe method for processing low-acid food, meats, fish, and vegetables. (Although you can also pressure-can fruit, the elaborate process of heating and cooling for such short processing times is inefficient. When appropriate, as it is for fruit, water-bath processing saves both time and fuel.) Here are the steps:

1. Place the pressure canner, containing its wire basket, on a cold stovetop element.

2. Refer to your manual to determine how much water to add to the canner to begin.

3. Place filled jars, tops screwed on, in the wire basket.

4. Tightly secure the lid on the pressure canner according to instructions.

5. Check the petcock valves with a toothpick or fine wire to determine that they are clear.

6. Turn on the heat under the canner and watch for steam; when it appears, begin timing and maintain a steady flow of steam for 10 minutes. This exhausting or venting of the canner is air leaving the jars and canner. If the canner isn't properly exhausted, the air will cause the reading on the gauge to be inaccurate, and your canning temperatures may be too low to be safe.

7. After the canner has exhausted for 10 minutes, close the vent or place the weight control over the steam valve.

8. Watch for the pressure gauge to reach the correct pressure (this is the time to make altitude adjustments—add ½ pound pressure for every additional 1,000 feet above sea level; refer to the instructions that came with your canner). Then set your timer and begin the designated processing time (see chart, opposite). Refer to the "Processing Times for Pressure Canning" table for general guidelines. Adjust the heat source so the gauge stays at the correct pressure called for in your recipe. Half-pint jars and smaller are processed in the same way as pints.

9. When jars have been processed for the correct amount of time, move the pressure canner off the heat and let it cool completely. *Caution: The canner will be very hot; protect yourself with oven mitts and pot holders.*

10. The steam and heat inside even a "cool" canner can be dangerous. Wait until the pressure gauge has gone down to zero, or until you can no longer see steam coming from the vent. On average it takes 45 to 60 minutes for the pressure to go down in a pressure canner.

11. Open the petcock slowly or remove the weighted gauge (remember, it's hot!). Unlock the canner lid and slide it across the top of the canner toward you, letting any remaining hot steam escape from the far side of the canner. Allow the canner to sit without its lid for 10 minutes before removing the jars.

PROCESSING TIMES FOR PRESSURE CANNING

Food	Pack	Processing Time at 10 Pounds Pressure (in minutes)		Headspace
		Pint	Quart	
Asparagus	Hot or raw	30	40	1 inch
Beans, snap	Hot or raw	20	25	1 inch
Beets	Hot	30	35	1 inch
Carrots	Hot or raw	25	30	1 inch
Corn, cut from cob	Hot or raw	55	85	1 inch
Okra	Hot	25	40	1 inch
Peas, shelled	Hot or raw	40	45	1 inch
Peppers, hot and sweet	Hot	35	n/a	1 inch
Pumpkin and winter squash (chunked; do *not* purée)	Hot	55	90	1 inch
Tomatoes, whole in water	Hot	n/a	45	½ inch
Tomatoes, whole in juice	Hot	n/a	25	½ inch
Tomato juice	Hot	15	15	½ inch
Tomato, sauce	Hot	15	15	½ inch

Cooling and storage

1. Insulate the counter with a cutting board, cooling rack, or several layers of newspaper or towels to avoid breakage due to a temperature contrast between the hot jars and a cool surface.

2. Using the jar lifter, remove the jars from either the canning kettle or the pressure canner while they are still hot. Place the jars upright where they can fully cool and remain undisturbed for the next 12 to 24 hours, during which time the final seal will form.

    A vacuum develops within the jars as they begin to cool, often indicated by a "ping" as the canning lid is pulled downward and a seal is formed. Many home canners refer to this sound as a welcome indicator of a job well done. A fully sealed lid will not have any play or give to it when pressed. Some manufacturers have incorporated a "safety button" in the center of their lids that visibly flattens to indicate a good seal. Any jar that does not seal properly should be refrigerated immediately and used within a week.

3. When the jars are fully cooled after their resting period, remove the screw bands and clean off any remaining stickiness. Clearly label the jars with their contents and their processing date.

4. Store the canned goods in a dry, cool, dark area for the best quality retention.

HOW LONG WILL CANNED FOOD KEEP?

Canned food is safe to eat as long as the seal holds. However, with each passing year some of the food's quality—its color, texture, taste, and nutritional value—is lost. For the greatest return on your efforts, both in flavor and nutrition, plan to consume your canned goods within a 6- to 8-month period. At that point the next growing season will be fully under way and the preserving cycle can begin again.

If at any point during storage a jar should lose its seal, indicated by some give in the lid, you should immediately discard its contents. A jar with an intact seal will "pop" when its lid is removed, indicating the vacuum has been broken. If there is any doubt or the food has developed an "off" or sour odor, *do not taste it*; discard the contents immediately.

DRYING

Drying foods in the open air with the warmth of the sun is humankind's oldest preservation method. Simple in concept and requiring little in the way of specialized equipment, drying foods is an economical and efficient way to process and store food. Shelf life is not contingent on an outside energy source, and dried foods require less space and weigh less than foods preserved in any other manner. The advantages that made this form of food preservation crucial for early nomadic populations are also attractive features for today's apartment or condo dweller who has little additional storage space.

Properly dried foods have had approximately 75 to 90 percent of their moisture removed. In the absence of moisture, organisms responsible for spoilage are unable to survive and grow. Thus dried provisions remain shelf stable for anywhere from a couple of months to a year, depending on their final moisture content, which varies depending on what food was dried and proper handling.

DRYING METHODS

Air dry: Hang bundles of herbs or set trays of food to dry in a warm dark area with good air circulation. A warm attic, an interior room away from the window, an outdoor shed, even the trunk of a car (when it's not running) are all possibilities.

Sun dry: The hot, dry conditions of a mid- or southwestern summer day are perfect to capture the sun's energy for drying with no expense or risk of burning or scorching. Set up drying trays in an area of full sun with good air circulation. At the end of each day take the trays indoors for the night to avoid dew. Set them out again the next sunny morning, repeating the process until the food is dried. Fruits can be dried nicely at 85°F or higher, but a temperature of 100°F or more is best for drying

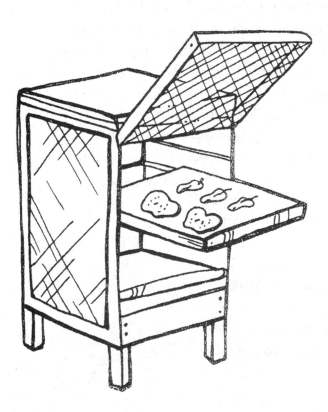

vegetables. Protect food drying outdoors from insects by draping with lightweight cotton cloth or nylon netting held up to keep it from coming in contact with sticky foods. *Note: Don't dry outdoors where there is traffic pollution, to avoid possible airborne lead contamination!*

Electric dehydrator: A good investment if you plan to do much drying. Look for a low-wattage dehydrator designed for power and space efficiency, with an accurate thermostat and a strong, but not too noisy fan. A good electric dehydrator is fairly foolproof in that you can load it up and forget about it, save for checking the food once a day to monitor its progress.

Oven drying: This is an effective method for drying small batches laid out on a wire cooling rack on a sheet pan. The challenge with oven drying is maintaining a low, steady temperature of 120 to 150°F. Warmer than that and food will cook, not dry. A reliable oven thermometer placed at the rear of your top tray will help gauge the proper heat setting. Prop the oven door open to promote good air circulation; if you have a convection oven with an internal fan, be sure that the fan will work with the door open.

GENERAL INSTRUCTIONS

1. **Harvest:** Harvest your fruit or vegetables at the peak of flavor. Begin the drying process as soon as possible to preserve flavor, color, and nutrients.

2. **Clean and prepare:** Wash food to completely remove any surface dirt. Peel, slice, shell, or otherwise prepare vegetables for drying. Foods cut into small pieces or thinly sliced will better retain their color and taste. Because vegetables are low in acid and spoil more easily, they need to dry quickly to avoid spoiling.

3. **Pretreatment:** Procedures that interrupt enzyme activity ensure that dried foods maintain their flavor, color, and nutrient levels and add to the shelf stability of the finished product (see page 21).

4. **Loading trays:** Spread vegetables or fruit on drying trays in a single layer. Allow room between pieces for air to circulate. Work with foods that will dry in the same amount of time; process strong-smelling foods, like onions, in a separate batch. When drying look-alike herbs and fruit leathers, label them before drying.

5. **Drying:** Set trays in the sun, a warm attic, or your dehydrator or oven. The drying temperature must be high enough that food will dry before it spoils, but low enough that it doesn't cook or get hard on the outside while remaining damp inside. Within those limits, the faster a food dries, the better its final quality.

6. **Turn or stir food as it dries:** Turn large pieces or stir smaller chunks two or three times a day to speed drying and prevent sticking. When using a dehydrator, place trays of moist foods at the top, rotating trays of almost-dried foods to the bottom shelves. Pieces around tray edges tend to dry first; remove them to prevent scorching. As the pieces shrink, consolidate on the trays to save space.

7. **Finishing:** Dry vegetables until they are brittle and the dried slices crumble or break when bent. Fruits are dry enough when their texture is somewhere between leathery and brittle. Some fruits, such as figs, cherries, raisins, and dates, remain sticky because of their sugar content, no matter how dry.

Fruit

Pretreat with an antioxidant to prevent browning and to preserve vitamins A and C (see page 22). After treatment, be sure to drain food well and pat dry before proceeding with drying. *Note: The use of sulfur to preserve home-dried food is not recommended.*

Vegetables

To avoid increasing water content, vegetables should be steam blanched before drying, to preserve nutrients and color (see page 20). Drain thoroughly and pat dry with towels to remove all surface water. You do not need to blanch chili peppers, onions, celery, zucchini slices, thinly sliced mushrooms, and garlic.

Meat

The principles for drying meat are the same as for those foods just discussed. Reduce moisture to arrest spoilage. Small uniform pieces, carefully controlled temperatures, and good air circulation are critical. The addition of a salt and sugar cure further ensures a safely preserved product.

Herbs

Harvest herbs just before flowering, when their essential oil content and flavor are highest. The night before you intend to harvest, hose off the plants to wash any grit or dust from their leaves. Cut plants after the morning dew has dried but before the heat of the afternoon sun dissipates the flavorful oils. Bundle stems into small bunches and hang them upside down in an airy, warm place out of direct sunlight. Once the leaves are crisp and dry, remove them by stripping from the stems; store in a dark container away from heat, light, and moisture. To use, crush the leaves between your hands to release their pungent tastes and aromas; plan to use within 6 months for the fullest flavor.

The best herbs for drying include: anise seed, bay, calendula petals, chamomile, dill and fennel seed, hop flowers, lavender, lemon balm, lemon verbena, marjoram, mint, mustard seed, oregano, rosemary, sage, savory, scented geranium, and thyme.

HOMEMADE DRYING TRAYS AND OUTDOOR DRYER

Create portable drying trays by stretching a single thickness of nylon netting or plastic screening over frames of soft lumber and stapling around the edges. Consider the inside dimensions of your oven when building frames; this will increase flexibility for their use indoors and out. Short 3- to 4-inch legs at each corner of the frame allow it to be stacked for efficiency or raised to maximize air circulation. You can fashion a very effective insect-proof, sun-powered dryer by creating a box-like structure on four legs with screened sides, top, and bottom. Hinge the top for easy access to the stacks of drying trays within. *Note: Don't ever lay food directly on galvanized screens; these contain toxic zinc and cadmium.*

STORAGE

Dried food will mold and spoil in the presence of excess moisture. This can be a particular problem in damp climates. After food has dried, before packaging, prepare it for long-term storage by one of the following two methods:

- ▶ **Conditioning** allows excess moisture from some pieces to be distributed among and absorbed by drier ones to equalize the moisture content within a batch. Empty trays of dried food into a large open container, cover with a light cloth or mesh to keep insects out, and place it in a warm, well-ventilated area. For the next week or two, stir the contents of the bowl once or twice a day.

- ▶ **Pasteurization** uses heat or cold to kill bacteria or insect eggs that would cause the dried food to spoil. Because air- or sun-drying food is less temperature controlled than other preservation methods, it is recommended that these be pasteurized with heat or cold before storage. Using heat, place dried food on trays and place in a 175°F oven for 10 to 15 minutes. For greater nutrient preservation, place plastic bags containing dried food into a zero-degree freezer for 2 to 4 days. *Note: You must use a deep freeze; the freezer compartment of a refrigerator does not get cold enough.*

Package finished dried food promptly in small serving-size quantities; once a package is opened, its contents should be used up quickly. Completely fill glass jars and squeeze excess air from zip-locking plastic storage bags, as light, moisture, and air will degrade dried food. Label and date the packages and store in a cool, dry, dark place. Dried food, properly handled, should remain in prime condition for at least 6 months.

"LIVE" STORAGE— AN OLD-FASHIONED ROOT CELLAR

Using "live" storage reduces dependence on electricity, requires little to no equipment, and takes some pressure off kitchen preserving duties. It is the easiest form of preservation. Cool, dark, moist conditions arrest enzyme action that leads to overripening, while an appropriate level of air circulation fends off decay. Under the proper light, temperature, humidity, and air circulation, food can be maintained and stored in a "live" condition. Requiring nothing in the way of processing or energy, live storage is a straightforward and economical solution to food preservation if you have space and can maintain the appropriate conditions.

HOW TO CREATE LIVE STORAGE

Use your imagination when considering live storage opportunities. Most unfinished or partially finished basements with concrete, tile, or linoleum floors—which are usually cluttered with bikes, boxes, camping equipment, and perhaps the laundry—can be easily modified to accommodate live storage conditions. Partition an area away from any heat source such as the furnace, appliances such as a freezer or washer and dryer, and sun from a window. To roughly determine humidity levels, place a small mirror against a wall. If after a few hours condensation appears on the mirror, indicated by water droplets or fog, the space is damp and may be adapted for live storage. A hygrometer or humidity gauge will give you a specific and accurate reading. Moist conditions— 90 to 95 percent humidity—are good for storing potatoes and many other crops. However, excessive humidity, indicated by water droplets on the surface of the food, will encourage mold and decay. Sixty to 75 percent humidity is considered dry storage, excellent for some live storage as well as pickles, jams, and canned goods, dried beans and grain (even storage of documents, holiday ornaments, and off-season clothes). Refer to the live storage guidelines chart (page 55) for specific requirements.

Your storage space may be room-sized or simply a large closet or pantry. Insulate the walls to further protect the space from outside heat, and cover any windows to block out light. Line the walls with shelving, and to promote air circulation, keep storage containers off the floor with removable, wooden slat flooring. A reliable thermometer and routine monitoring will help you know when to regulate storage temperature by ventilating doors, windows, or other openings. To maintain humidity, routinely dampen the wooden flooring or set out pans of heavily salted water (the salt in the water prevents the formation of unwanted molds and bacteria). In extremely moist climates, or in the absence of a window you can open, you may need a fan to provide additional air circulation.

Warm conditions may be found in an attic, heated garage, spare closet, or pantry space—even under the bed. A well-ventilated basement under a house with central heating generally has a temperature range of 50 to 60°F, good for ripening tomatoes and short-term storage of pumpkins, winter squash, sweet potatoes, and onions. *Note: Don't store live food in or near a garage, unless it is wrapped so that it will be fully protected from harmful car emissions.*

Cool condition requirements are easy to accommodate in an unheated basement or garage, outdoor shed, or rented storage unit; even an out-of-season trailer can be modified for short-term food storage. Many old houses have dirt floor cellars, harkening back to a day when food storage was a routine practicality. Typically these cellars have an outside entrance and at least one window that can be used to ventilate and control storage temperatures. Storing vegetables and fruits in outbuildings is practical only where the climate is consistently cold but the average temperature is not below freezing. Monitor the interior temperature of these separate storage spaces carefully when severe cold is forecast, and be ready to add supplemental heat or extra insulation to protect your stored foods.

Other storage possibilities

Traditional root cellar: The secret to a good root cellar is a combination of insulation from outside air and a design that allows it to absorb warmth from the ground via a dirt floor. Typical root cellar instructions assume outdoor temperatures during winter that average 30°F or lower. Cellars constructed at least in part below ground hold an optimum temperature longer and more uniformly than cellars built above ground. Double wall construction, a flue for summer venting, and adequate protection from rodents are critical design considerations.

Buried storage: A wooden barrel, box, or a galvanized can with a lid can be filled with food and buried to form a sort of mini root cellar. Make sure the container hasn't held anything that could poison or give an off flavor to the food, and never use drums or containers that might have held pesticides or other chemicals. Buried outdoor storage has the disadvantage of being somewhat inconvenient to access. Furthermore, once a pit is opened, its entire contents should be removed and used within 1 to 2 weeks. For this reason, it's better to construct several small pits rather than one large one; this allows you access to what you need as you need it.

To create buried storage:

▶ Dig a hole and line the bottom with rock to keep the container from resting directly on soil.

▶ Make several holes in the bottom of the storage container to allow for drainage, and set the can on top of the rocks. The upper rim of the container should be 2 inches above ground level.

▶ Carefully pack vegetables into the can, with straw or leaves separating each layer from the next. You may combine different vegetables, provided they require the same storage conditions.

▶ Cover the top of the can with a mound of insulating material—such as straw, hay, or dried leaves—that is at least 1 or 2 feet deep and that extends at least a foot out from the sides of the can.

In-garden storage: It is possible to leave some root crops, such as carrots, turnips, and parsnips, in place in the garden for part or all of the winter. Some root crops actually improve in flavor, becoming sweeter after a light freeze as their starches convert to sugar. Cover root crops with a foot or more of straw, hay, dried leaves, or other light mulch once the ground is thoroughly chilled or begins to freeze in late fall. Mulching too early, when the soil is still warm, will cause vegetables to rapidly decay. Root vegetables will remain unharmed unless the temperature around the roots gets down to 25°F or lower, although they can be difficult to dig out of frozen ground. Where rodents are a garden nuisance, it is wiser to store crops in a buried closed container or in an indoor storage area. Other cold-hardy crops—such as beets, cabbage, Chinese cabbage, cauliflower, celery, endive, cos or romaine lettuce, kale, leeks, and onions—will endure early light frosts and can be stored in the garden for several weeks or more under mulch.

TIPS FOR SUCCESSFUL LIVE STORAGE:

▶ Harvest during dry weather; wet produce is much more susceptible to spoilage in storage. Handle food carefully to prevent skin cuts and bruises, which also invite decay. Adhering to the old "one bad apple will spoil the barrel" maxim, make sure there are no crushed, cut, or decaying foods mixed in with those to be stored. Don't wash produce before storing; for optimal results, chill foods before placing them into cold storage.

▶ At least once a year, remove all containers from your storeroom for a thorough cleaning. Wash down the walls and ceiling before you replenish the space.

▶ Suitable storage containers include sturdy food-quality plastic containers with airtight lids, wooden crates, sturdy cardboard boxes, Styrofoam coolers, baskets, metal and plastic trash cans without a lid, mesh bags, and plastic stacking bins. Lidded tins made for food storage are especially good for storing dried beans, cereals, and flours.

▶ Make sure your storage site is accessible for regular maintenance and monitoring. You must check the condition of stored food on a regular basis. The least bit of decay can quickly spread to contaminate your stores. At the first sign of a problem, remove the affected fruit or vegetable and salvage whatever is possible of the unaffected produce by another means of preserving or by eating at once whatever you are certain is safe. To allow for losses during storage, you should put away more than you expect to need.

LIVE STORAGE GUIDELINES					
Fruits/ Vegetables	Cold: 32 to 40°F	Warm: 55 to 70°F	Humidity	Shelf life (in months)	Notes
Apples	x		Moist	4–6	Provide air circulation; wrap fruits in newspaper or layer in straw
Citrus	x		Moist	1½	
Grapes	x		Moist	1–2	Store in shallow containers cushioned with packing material to avoid crushing
Pears	x		Moist	3	Provide air circulation; wrap fruits in newspaper or layer in straw
Beets	x		Moist	3–5	Remove green tops and layer in damp sand or sawdust
Cabbage	x		Moist	2–4	Remove outer leaves and wrap in newspaper
Carrots	x		Moist	6	Remove green tops and layer in damp sand or sawdust
Cauliflower	x		Moist	1½–3	Keep the leaves intact; store in covered boxes
Celery	x		Moist	1–2	Stand upright in moist sand
Dried beans/peas	x		Dry	Indefinite	Store in airtight lidded containers
Endive	x		Moist	2–3	Keep the roots and leaves intact; store upright in moist sand or soil

LIVE STORAGE GUIDELINES *continued*

Fruits/ Vegetables	Cold: 32 to 40°F	Warm: 55 to 70°F	Humidity	Shelf life (in months)	Notes
Onions	x		Dry	4–6	Cure in a warm location, then braid tops and hang or store in a suspended mesh bag
Potatoes	x		Moist	4–6	Store in a covered box away from all light
Pumpkins and winter squash		x	Dry	4–6	Wash with a mild bleach solution before storing
Root crops	x		Moist	2–4	Remove green tops and layer in damp sand or sawdust
Sweet potatoes		x	Dry	4–6	
Tomatoes (mature green)		x	Dry	1–1½	Wash and dry without stems; store in a single layer to prevent crushing and monitor daily

OTHER CURES

VINEGAR

Pickling is probably the most common method of preserving with vinegar. The term *pickle* has come to be synonymous with cucumber pickles; in fact, most vegetables and some fruits as well as certain meats and eggs can also be preserved by pickling. Relishes, chutneys, ketchup, and flavored vinegars are based, at least in part, on the preservative qualities of vinegar.

Most foods are pickled by pouring a hot spiced vinegar solution over prepared ingredients. The process is often combined with salt, sugar, or both for additional flavor and keeping qualities, although it is the acetic acid naturally present in vinegar that serves as the primary preservative. Vinegar replaces the moisture in pickled food and stops the growth of dangerous microorganisms, which would lead to spoilage. Vinegar must contain 4 to 6 percent acetic acid to effectively serve as a preservative; most store-bought vinegars are well within these parameters and may safely be used. Do not use homemade vinegar for pickling unless you have a means of accurately determining its acidity.

It is important to carefully follow pickling recipe instructions to maintain the proper acidity for safe shelf storage. If you find the finished pickles to be too sour or tart, you can add a small amount of sugar to the recipe to buffer the flavor, but do not reduce or dilute the amount of vinegar called for in the recipe. Finished pickles may be refrigerated for short-term storage or canned in a hot-water bath for long-term storage.

SUGAR

Although hardly the stuff of daily sustenance, sweetened fruit spreads, syrups, and sugared preserves allow us to keep seasonal treats for enjoyment throughout the year. These are foods of pleasure and celebration that bring sweet satisfaction to festive holiday meals and the humble breakfast table alike. Prepared with care, packaged and labeled with imagination, these simple everyday luxuries make beautiful and always appreciated gifts.

Sugar is often added to recipes to extend keeping properties as well as for its added sweetness. As sugar is mixed with fresh food, the natural moisture content of the food becomes saturated with the sweetener to create an inhospitable environment for the growth of harmful microbes. At concentrations of 50 to 60 percent, sugar begins to have preserving properties; above 70 percent, all microorganism growth is halted.

White cane sugar, brown sugar, molasses, honey, and maple syrup may all be used in varying amounts—and will impart differing flavors—to preserve fruits, jams, and jellies, and even a few vegetables that lend themselves to a sweetening treatment.

HONEY

Pure honey is an example of a food being "preserved in sugar"; it will keep indefinitely without further preserving. Over time honey will crystallize or granulate to form a stiff, whitened, sugary mixture. Storing liquid honey under cool temperatures will hasten this process. Crystallization does not affect flavor or nutrition in any way; in fact, many people appreciate the spreadable consistency it imparts. To reliquefy honey, slowly warm the container in a double boiler or microwave just until the honey has cleared. Do not allow honey to boil, as that will alter the flavor and reduce its naturally healthful properties.

The sweetness of honey is more concentrated than that of sugar, so it may be used in smaller quantities to achieve the same degree of sweetening. In addition to sweetness, honey adds its own unique flavor to any recipe. This may be delicately floral or a stronger, more pungent flavor, depending on the source of the honey.

DOUSING IN ALCOHOL

The succulent marriage of ripe fruit, sugar, and complementary spirits has long been a favored preserving custom. *Tutti-frutti* or *rumtopf*, more a kitchen tradition than an actual recipe, dates back hundreds of years. As fresh ripe fruit is picked over the summer harvest season, it is layered in a large glass or ceramic crock with an equal dry measure of sugar for each addition and topped up with brandy, rum, or other form of alcohol; other fruits, harvested in their prime, may be added to the crock as the season progresses. At the end of the summer, the now-full crock is carefully set aside in a cool, dark location to mellow and age.

The resulting heady preserves are served with cake, custard, ice cream or on their own. The remaining flavorful elixir may be used as a dessert sauce, added to other beverages, or enjoyed as a delicious after-dinner cordial, perfectly capturing a summertime pleasure and transforming it into a fruity essence for sipping on a winter's evening by the fire.

Spirits that are at least 40 percent alcohol by volume (80 proof) serve as an effective preservative by permeating the food and inhibiting the growth of dangerous bacteria; fruits give up their juices to flavor the spirit in an exchange of fluids. You can include the rind, skin, or pits of the fruit to add another dimension of flavor—apricot, peaches, and other stone fruit pits lend a bitter almond taste, and citrus rinds are saturated with aromatic essential oils. The alcohol serves as a solvent, drawing out flavor; sugar, either dry or in syrup form, is added to counter the tendency of alcohol to toughen the skins and shrink the fruit, as well as to sweeten and mellow the final product.

Spirited herbal infusions were first crafted by monks in the middle ages as curative tonics; today they enjoy a newly revived popularity in

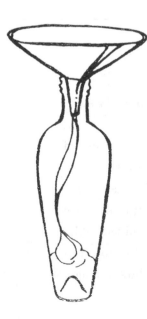

trendy cocktails. In the same way that spirits capture the syrupy, lush character of fruit, savory chilies and herbs may be steeped in alcohol to create spicy and aromatic condiments, the most common being hot pepper sauce.

Even those who are challenged for storage space— no room in the freezer or kitchen pantry—or who have little inclination to fuss with the canning process can still preserve the flavors of summer with homemade alcohol-based infusions, extracts, schnapps, and heady desserts.

SALT

The golden age of exploration would have yielded far fewer discoveries without the sustaining nourishment and scurvy-preventing properties of salt-cured foods. Perhaps the oldest and most primitive curing method, salt remains an effective way to preserve foods. Fundamentally a rock, salt is a mineral derived from salt water or mined on land. It is a component of our very blood and vitally necessary for our bodies to function. That culinary standard, *Joy of Cooking*, states, "The interplay of salt and water is essential to life itself."

Salt draws moisture out of food by osmosis; food is preserved when unwanted microorganisms cannot survive in the resulting moisture-deprived environment. Bacteria cannot survive in a 25-percent saline solution; a more palatable 10-percent solution is commonly used to arrest spoilage in food. Salt can be applied either dry or in a solution, called *brine*. A dry cure mixture of salt, often tempered with sugar and other seasonings, is generously rubbed directly onto a food's surface. Moisture is extracted and the surface salt dissolves into a solution that infuses back into the food, bringing its preservative qualities with it. Brining involves submerging food in a saline solution—again, often enhanced with sugar, spices, and other aromatics. Liquid brine penetrates food more quickly than a dry rub to cure and preserve, while at the same time serving as a delivery vehicle for other flavors. Ham, olives, cheese, sauerkraut, fermented pickles, beef jerky, corned meats, gravlax or lox, and preserved lemons are just a few of the foods whose preservation and very character are determined primarily by salt.

FAT AND OIL

Lard, butter, and other fats that are solid at room temperature can be used to preserve food by forming an air-tight, moisture-proof barrier between the finished dish and the exterior environment. Remember, time doesn't spoil food—microbes do. Robbing microorganisms of the air and moisture they need to flourish halts their activity and thus holds food in a preserved state under the right conditions—namely cool or cold surroundings.

SMOKE

Smoke acidifies the surface of any food it comes in contact with, providing a slight preservative effect by creating an environment inhospitable to unwanted microorganisms. Although at one time smoke was an actual method of preserving, today it is more commonly used to enhance flavor in meat, fish, cheese, and other foods.

PART TWO

RECIPES: BEYOND THE BASICS

Brilliantly colored, wholesome fruits and vegetables in all their rich variety are the foundation of a healthy diet. Government studies conducted by the United States Department of Agriculture, the United States Department of Health and Human Services, and the National Academy of Sciences recommend five to ten servings of fruits and vegetables a day to maintain optimum energy, strength, and general well-being. The emergence of regional farmers markets, community supported agriculture (CSA) share programs, and a newly rediscovered interest in vegetable gardening all have broadened our experience and developed our taste for an ever-expanding range of clean, organic, nourishing food. Well beyond the standard peas, corn, and carrots, we're exploring Asian vegetables, fava beans, and vitamin-rich greens, colorful squashes and heirloom tomatoes, for a diet that is not only good for us but tastes good too.

Frozen, canned, jammed, pickled, bottled, or dried, preserves are not a substitute for fresh food. Instead, they enhance flavor and add complexity and interest to fall and winter meals that would otherwise become pallid shadows of the more productive seasons. Who wouldn't choose a rich, hearty tomato sauce over disappointing, flavorless out-of-season tomatoes? Sweet luscious jams and jellies take summer berries to new heights, and frozen or dried corn—admittedly a departure from summer-dining bliss—adds texture and tooth to baked goods, winter soups, and stews.

There was a time when many families kept their own dairy cow; today, it is a rare household that maintains one. For most, the enormous burden of feeding and daily care, complications of disease and disposition, not to mention issues with land use and waste disposal make the practice prohibitive. However, an ever-increasing number of small, multidimensional family farms are springing up in the suburbs, while within town limits where zoning allows, more and more resourceful, inventive urban pioneers are raising miniature dairy goats, and the backyard chicken movement is flourishing.

Fortunately, for those of us less inclined toward animal husbandry, local, organic, rich, and oh-so-fresh milk, eggs, and even cheese as well as organic, pastured meats and local seafood are among the goods offered alongside fresh-picked produce, baked goods, and fresh flowers at neighborhood farmers markets, food co-ops, and even forward-thinking grocery stores. We have a delicious opportunity to support not just our own pursuit of a seasonal healthy diet but also the work of local dairies and ranchers.

FRUIT

SWEETENED FRUIT PRESERVES

Transforming fresh fruit into delicious, sweet spreads is a summer tradition many cooks look forward to, just as their friends and families
anticipate savoring the luscious results throughout the rest of the year.

Jams and jellies, sauces, butters, and syrups are all, in one form
or another, a mixture of fruit and sugar. Most are boiled to thicken;
uncooked freezer jams and dessert sauces, which retain their fresh
fruit flavor and brilliant color, are an exception. Jam contains sliced or
puréed fruit; jelly is made from fruit juice. Setting to a proper gelled
consistency depends on a correct balance of fruit, sugar, acid, and pectin. Most jam recipes call for a 2:1 ratio of fruit to sugar by weight or
volume; jelly recipes call for a 1:1 ratio of sugar to juice. Do not try to
double or triple jam and jelly recipes; the additional cooking time will
not only impact the flavor but also break down the pectin and prevent
it from setting.

PECTIN

This natural substance, which is found in fruit, gels when heated with acid and sugar. Natural ripening causes pectin to break down—consequently, overripe fruit will not set properly. Most jam and jelly recipes include at least some slightly under-ripe fruit for their added pectin content. To achieve a gelled consistency, you can either combine pectin-rich fruits with those containing lesser amounts, use commercially prepared pectin, or make your own homemade pectin solution.

▶ **High pectin fruits:** Sour (unripe) apples, crab apples, cranberries, currants, grapes (with skins), lemons, logan-berries, sour plums, quince, and green gooseberries

▶ **Medium pectin fruits:** Ripe apples, blackberries, oranges, grapefruit, sour cherries, and grape juice

▶ **Low pectin fruits:** Apricots, peaches, figs, prunes, pears, strawberries, and raspberries

To test the pectin level in fruit juice, combine 1 tablespoon fruit juice with 1 tablespoon rubbing alcohol in a glass container. With adequate pectin, the fruit juice will turn into a jelly-like mass that can be scooped up with a spoon. If pectin is too low, the juice will not gel and you'll know to add more. *Note: Rubbing alcohol is toxic; do not eat this test mixture.*

Jelly or jam made with added commercial pectin requires less cooking and generally produces a larger yield. The result is a prod-uct with more vibrant, natural fruit flavor. Packaged pectin may be powdered or liquid. For successful results, carefully follow the directions for whichever pectin you are using. In recent years a low-methoxyl or no-sugar pectin has come on the market, which gels fruit without using sugar in the recipe. However, preserves made without sugar do not have as long a shelf life once they have thawed or been opened. *Note: Buy fresh packaged pectin each year; old pectin may not gel properly.*

Finally, homemade pectin from apples can be used when making jam or jelly with low-pectin fruit juice. In a large stockpot, boil together 2 cups water for every 1 pound of apple slices for 45 minutes, stirring occasionally. Pour the apple pulp into a strainer lined with a single layer of dampened cheesecloth or a jelly bag to drain; discard the pulp. Boil the resulting extracted juice for 15 minutes: the result is apple pectin or *jelly stock*. Use 1 cup of it for every 1 cup of low-pectin fruit juice. Add ¾ cup of sugar for every cup of liquid (combined jelly stock and fruit juice) used in the recipe. Freeze any unused pectin for future use.

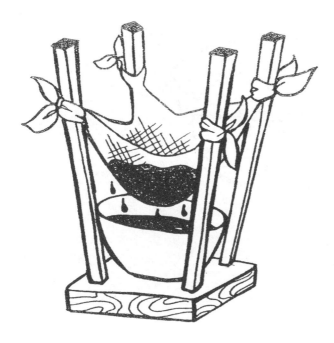

Equipment

In addition to the jars and equipment listed for water-bath canning (see page 34), the following items are helpful when making jams, jellies, and other sweet preserves:

- ▶ Food mill or potato ricer (for crushing fruit and removing skins and seeds)
- ▶ Candy or food thermometer
- ▶ Kitchen scale (to more accurately measure fruit and sugar by weight)
- ▶ Preserving pan (copper is traditional, but heavy enamel or stainless steel is also good at conducting an even heat; a wide open surface facilitates evaporation and reduces cooking time)
- ▶ Jelly bag or cheesecloth and colander
- ▶ Wooden spoons or silicone spatulas (will not heat up when stirring hot mixtures)

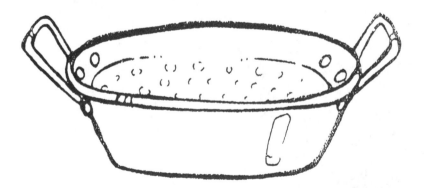

CHUNKY PEACH JAM

Whether spread on buttered toast at breakfast, basted on a holiday ham, or spooned over vanilla ice cream, you'll love the luscious fruit flavor.

Season: Mid- to late summer
Yield: 6 cups
Store: Cool, dark pantry

6 cups peeled, pitted, coarsely chopped firm-ripe peaches
    (about 3 pounds)
5 cups sugar
4 to 6 tablespoons lemon juice

Combine the peaches, sugar, and 4 tablespoons of the lemon juice in a preserving pan. Taste and add more lemon juice as needed to make the fruit pleasantly tart. Heat the mixture over medium heat and stir to dissolve the sugar. Cook the jam until it reaches 220°F on a kitchen thermometer or otherwise passes the jelly-doneness test (see page 76). Remove from heat.

Carefully ladle the hot jam into hot, sterilized pint or half-pint jars, allowing ¼ inch headspace. Follow water-bath canning instructions (page 34) and process for 10 minutes.

Variation: Crack 6 peach pits and add the nutty kernels to the boiling jam for a subtle almond flavor. Divide the pits among the jars before filling. Nectarines, apricots, or plums may be substituted for the peaches. Rather than peeling the apricots or plums, process to a coarse purée in a food processor before cooking.

NO-COOK STRAWBERRY FREEZER JAM

The perfect project when the kitchen is too hot to consider turning on the stove—or freeze the berries (page 16) and do a stovetop jam later, when the weather cools.

Season: Mid- to late summer
Yield: 3 to 4 cups
Store: Freezer (6 to 9 months)

4 cups crushed strawberries (about 3 pints)
4 cups sugar (divided)
2 tablespoons lemon juice
1 package (1¾ ounce) powdered pectin

Layer the strawberries, 3 cups of the sugar, and lemon juice in a mixing bowl and fold gently to combine. Let stand at room temperature while the sugar dissolves, about 2 hours.

Combine the pectin and remaining sugar; slowly add to the now juicy mixture and let it stand for another 30 minutes, stirring occasionally to keep everything well mixed.

Pour the finished jam into jars or freezer containers, allowing ½ inch headspace, and seal. Refrigerate for 24 hours to fully set; transfer to freezer for long-term storage.

Variations: Substitute blueberries, blackberries, or raspberries for the strawberries; particularly seedy berries may be put through a sieve or food mill before mixing with the sugar. Taste for a good sugar/acid balance; some berries may require a bit more lemon juice.

ALMOST-SEEDLESS BLACKBERRY JAM

Fully ripe blackberries, although low in natural pectin and remarkably seedy, are filled with luscious flavor and a sweet perfume. In this recipe, apples contribute the necessary pectin, the seeds are removed, and the lemon juice nicely balances the flavor with a welcome tartness. Summer in a jar!

Season: Late summer
Yield: 6 cups
Store: Cool, dark pantry

6 cups ripe blackberries, picked over, rinsed, and drained
   (about 3½ pints)
2½ cups coarsely chopped tart apples, including skins and cores
1½ to 2 cups water
Approximately 5 cups sugar
3 tablespoons lemon juice, or to taste

Crush the berries with a potato masher or whirl briefly in a food processor.

Place the crushed berries, apples, and 1½ cups of the water in a preserving pan. Cook the mixture over medium heat, uncovered, until the fruit is very soft, 15 to 20 minutes. Stir often, adding additional water to keep the fruit from sticking.

Put the hot fruit through a food mill or fine strainer set over a bowl to remove the seeds. Rinse out the preserving pan.

Measure the remaining fruit pulp into the preserving pan and add 1 cup sugar for every cup of fruit; taste, adding enough lemon juice to make the fruit pleasantly tart.

Heat the mixture over medium-high heat to bring it rapidly to a boil, stirring constantly until the sugar dissolves. Cook the jam until it reaches 220°F on a kitchen thermometer or otherwise passes the jelly-doneness test (see page 76). Remove from heat.

Carefully ladle the hot jam into hot, sterilized pint or half-pint jars, allowing ¼ inch headspace. Follow the water-bath canning instructions (page 34) and process for 10 minutes.

PLUM JELLY

· ·

Most old neighborhoods seem to have at least one ancient plum tree, buzzing with yellow jackets and laden with fruit that goes unpicked. Don a protective long-sleeved shirt and brave the wasps for the makings of this beautiful jewel-toned jelly. Different varieties of plums will yield slightly different results as their natural pectin levels vary. Damson plums are very tart with acidic skins and are much higher in pectin than other plums, for example.

Season: Mid- to late summer

Yield: 6 cups

Store: Cool, dark pantry

· ·

4 pounds Italian prune plums, halved and pitted (at least
    ¼ of which should be barely ripe)

2 cups water

3 to 4 cups sugar

3 to 5 tablespoons lemon juice

Place the plums and water in a saucepan and bring to a boil. Simmer until the fruit is very soft, 15 to 20 minutes.

Transfer the fruit to a dampened jelly bag or cheesecloth-lined colander suspended over a bowl. Drain for several hours to fully extract the juices. The yield will be about 4 cups. Do not press on the fruit, squeeze the bag, or try to hurry the process in any way—if you do, you will cloud what should be a rosy-golden, crystal-clear juice.

Measure the strained juice into a preserving pan and add 1 cup of sugar for every cup of plum juice; taste, adding lemon juice to make the fruit pleasantly tart.

Heat the mixture over medium-high heat to bring it rapidly to a boil, stirring constantly until the sugar dissolves. Cook the jam until it reaches 220°F on a kitchen thermometer or otherwise passes the jelly-doneness test (see below). Remove from heat.

Carefully ladle the hot jelly into hot, sterilized half-pint jars, allowing ¼ inch headspace. Follow water-bath canning instructions (see below) and process for 10 minutes.

TESTING JELLY DONENESS

Temperature test: Using a jelly or candy thermometer, bring the mixture to 220°F (for high altitudes subtract 2 degrees for each 1,000 feet of elevation above sea level).

Sheet test: Dip a cool metal spoon into the boiling jelly mixture. Away from the heat, turn the spoon on its side. When the fruit mixture forms a single large drop or "sheets" off the spoon, the jelly is done.

Chilled saucer test: Place a small saucer in the freezer while you are preparing the jelly on the stovetop. Place 1 tablespoon of the hot jelly on the chilled saucer and return it to the freezer for a couple of minutes. The jellying point has been reached when you can divide the mixture by drawing a finger through the center.

FRUIT SAUCE AND BUTTER

Although applesauce is certainly the most familiar, any fruit may be preserved as a sauce, generally defined as a nonjelled fruit purée that is less sweet than a jam or jelly. Sauces are quick and easy to put up and may be frozen or canned for long-term storage.

Prepare the fruit (stem, peel, core, seed, and cut into smaller pieces) and put into a preserving pan with just enough water or fruit juice to prevent the fruit from sticking as it cooks, about ½ to 1 cup. Bring to a boil and simmer until the fruit is softened. Remove from heat and mash, strain, or purée to desired smoothness. Sample the purée and sweeten to taste with sugar, honey, or maple syrup; a dash of lemon juice may help to "spark" blandness.

Return the pan to the heat and gently simmer just until the sugar dissolves, stirring constantly to prevent sticking. Ladle the finished sauce into hot, sterilized jars or freezer containers and process for storage.

A fruit sauce, prepared in this way and further cooked down to reduce, is called a *butter*. Fruit butters have a thick, smooth, spreadable consistency, and their reduced sugar content gives them a more pure fruit flavor than a jam or jelly.

When preparing fruit butter, long, slow cooking at a low temperature with careful attention to stirring to avoid scorching is critical. Baking in a 300 to 350°F oven in a covered kettle, a slow cooker, or even microwaving are all easier alternatives to attentive stovetop cooking. Process the finished butter for long-term storage by canning or freezing or simply store under refrigeration for immediate enjoyment.

FRESH RASPBERRY COULIS

This quick-to-prepare, lightly sweetened purée is an easy way to process an abundant bumper crop and makes a delicious topping for decadent choco- late cake or simple rice pudding.

Season: Mid- to late summer
Yield: Variable
Store: Freezer (6 months)

Fresh raspberries, picked over, rinsed, and drained
Sugar or honey
Lemon juice

Simply mash, purée, and strain the raspberries. Sweeten the fruit to taste with sugar or honey and balance the flavors with the sparkle of lemon juice. Pack into containers, allowing ½ inch headspace. Follow instructions for freezing (see page 17).

Variation: For greater flexibility you may omit the sugar, using the purée in subsequent recipes, although this will shorten its freezer life to 3 months.

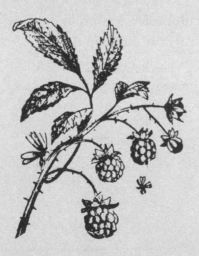

MICROWAVE APPLE BUTTER

This recipe does away with steamy hours spent stirring over a hot stove and the crushing disappointment when a carefully tended batch scorches in a moment of distraction.

Season: Late summer to fall
Yield: About 2 cups
Store: Refrigerator (2 months)

1½ pounds apples, quartered
½ cup lightly packed dark brown sugar
½ cup white sugar
½ teaspoon ground cinnamon
3 whole allspice berries
3 whole cloves
Pinch of freshly ground nutmeg
Generous pinch of kosher salt
1 tablespoon lemon juice

Combine all ingredients in a glass 11- by 8½- by 4-inch dish. Cover tightly with plastic wrap. Cook at 100°F for 15 minutes.

Remove from oven and purée the now softened fruit in a food processor; take care to avoid being burned by hot spatters. Press the purée through a fine sieve to remove any skins and the whole spices; cook, uncovered at 100°F for 10 minutes longer.

Remove from oven and pack the hot butter into hot, sterilized pint jars and cover with a tight lid. Let stand until cool and store refrigerated for up to 2 months.

Variation: To make 2 pints, double the amount of apples and sugar. Increase the spices to ¾ teaspoon ground cinnamon, 6 allspice berries, 5 cloves, and ¼ teaspoon freshly ground nutmeg. Cook in a 14- by 11- by 2-inch dish for 20 minutes. Process the fruit and cook the resulting purée for another 10 minutes before packing into containers. For long-term storage process the finished butter by canning or freezing.

QUINCE CHEESE (MEMBRILLO)

Not an actual cheese, but a translucent, thickened ruby purée or paste that jells hard enough to unmold and slice. Delicious on its own as a sweet after dinner, in Spain membrillo is a traditional accompaniment served with manchego, a semi-firm, slightly salty cheese made from sheep milk. The poise between sweet/salty and smooth/crumbly is heaven.

Season: Fall
Yield: About 3½ pounds
Store: Refrigerator (several months)

4 pounds ripe quince
4½ quarts water
1 vanilla bean, split
Zest and juice of 1 small lemon
Sugar

Scrub the quince to remove fuzz; cut out the blossom ends. Cut into thin slices including the skin and cores. Put in a preserving pan and cover generously with water. Add the vanilla bean and the lemon juice and zest and bring to a boil. Lower heat and simmer, partially covered, until the fruit is very soft, 45 minutes to 1½ hours depending on the fruit.

Set a colander over a mixing bowl and pour in the fruit and juice. Discard the vanilla bean and drain the pulp thoroughly. Transfer the pulp to a food processor or food mill and purée finely. Strain the pulp again to remove any fibrous bits.

Measure out and reserve 4 cups of the strained quince juice and refrigerate to later process into jelly or add to other kitchen preparations.

Measure the remaining juice and pulp into a rinsed-out preserving pan. Add 1 cup sugar for every cup of the mixture (for example, 4 cups juice and quince pulp requires 4 cups sugar). Bring the mixture to a boil and simmer, stirring almost constantly, until the purée becomes very thick—sometimes this can take 30 minutes, but watch closely should it take less time. The paste is done when the mixture pulls away from the edges of the pan and will hold a mounded shape when scooped with a spoon.

Remove the pan from the heat and allow the mixture to cool for a few minutes. Transfer the membrillo to a standing mixer fitted with a paddle attachment or beat with a hand mixer until it is almost completely cool. Pack the quince paste into shallow, small plastic containers with lids and store in the refrigerator.

Variation: Line a sheet pan with plastic wrap and spread the quince paste in an even layer. Let the paste sit out on the kitchen counter, uncovered, overnight to firm up. If the weather is damp you may need to dry it in a very low oven (100 to 120°F).

When the surface is only faintly tacky, cover with more plastic wrap and flip the sheet of quince paste; peel off the plastic that was on the bottom (now on top) and continue to dry until the paste is no longer sticky. Cut the paste into serving pieces and allow to dry a bit longer. Dust with confectioners' sugar and pack in an airtight container between layers of waxed paper.

AND MORE

Everyone knows jams, jellies, and butter are traditional ways to preserve fruit. However, lucious syrups, cordials, infused vinegars, and even pickles bring another dimension to meals and form the base for delectable beverages.

BLUEBERRY SYRUP

· ·

Full-bodied sweetened fruit syrups—sometimes referred to as fruit honeys—
may be poured over pancakes, ice cream, and other desserts. Mix with
sparkling water for a refreshing fruit soda or to create a base for creative
cocktails. This is a quick and efficient way to preserve an abundant harvest
when you don't have time for processing jam or jelly.

> **Season: Mid- to late summer**
> **Yield: Variable**
> **Store: Refrigerator (2 months)**

· ·

Fresh blueberries, picked over and rinsed
Water
3 cups sugar
Lemon juice

Put the fruit through a food mill or whirl briefly in a food processor to
a coarse purée. Measure the purée into a preserving pan, adding 1 cup
water for every 4 cups of fruit. Quickly bring to a simmer, reduce heat,
and cook for 5 minutes or until the fruit is completely softened; a brief
cooking period helps to retain the fresh fruit flavor.

Pour the hot mixture into a jelly bag or a colander lined with dampened cheesecloth and collect the juice as it drains in a heat-proof bowl.
Twist the bag or press the solids with a spoon to get as much juice as
possible from the purée. Discard the remaining pulp.

Prepare a sugar syrup by bringing 2 cups water and the sugar to a
boil, stirring until the sugar dissolves. Boil without stirring until the
syrup reaches 260°F on a kitchen thermometer; remove from heat.
Sweeten the blueberry juice with sugar syrup to taste, adding lemon

juice to balance flavors. Return the mixture to the pan and boil for 1 minute. Remove from heat and cool completely.

Syrup keeps well in the refrigerator or may be processed for 30 minutes in a water bath (page 34) for stable shelf storage.

Variation: Just about any ripe, juicy fruit with good flavor can be made into syrup following this procedure.

PICKLED CHERRIES

. . . .

This recipe not only produces a delicious accompaniment for sharp cheeses and cured meats but also provides the base for a fruity cherry-flavored vinegar. Dry-pack frozen cherries work splendidly; this may be the only reliable way to find tart pie cherries if you don't have a tree yourself or know a generous someone who does.

> **Season: Summer (any time if using frozen fruit)**
> **Yield: About 6 cups**
> **Store: Refrigerator or cool, dark pantry**

. . . .

> 2 pounds ripe firm sweet or pie cherries, stemmed and pitted
> 3 cups (or so) distilled white vinegar
> 4 cups sugar

Combine cherries and vinegar in a half-gallon glass jar or nonreactive bowl, making sure that the fruit is completely submerged. Cover tightly and allow to stand at cool room temperature for 3 days.

Drain off the now cherry-infused vinegar and reserve in a tightly capped bottle to keep out air (see recipe that follows).

Layer the drained cherries and sugar in a large jar or divide evenly between two quart-size canning jars, finishing with a layer of sugar. Thoroughly wipe clean the jar rim(s) and cap with new sterilized two-piece lid(s), hand-tightened securely.

Set the jar(s) in a cool spot where you will remember to gently shake them every day, inverting the jar so the dissolving sugar and cherries are evenly bathed in their juices. At the end of nine days the sugar will have completely turned to syrup.

Transfer the cherries and their syrup into sterilized pint canning jars and tighten their lids securely. Label the jars and store in a cool, dark place for 1 month, during which time the cherries will plump up and absorb most of the syrup. Store opened jars in the refrigerator.

FRUIT VINEGAR

* *

Jewel-toned fruity vinegars perk up salads and marinades and liven deglazing sauces for pork, duck, and chicken. Try a splash with fresh shucked oysters or mix several tablespoons with sparkling water over ice to create a shrub—an old-fashioned beverage that is particularly refreshing in hot weather.

> **Season: Summer through fall**
> **Yield: About 6 cups**
> **Store: Refrigerator or cool, dark pantry**

* *

Reserved cherry vinegar from pickled cherries
>   *OR*

Fruit
White wine vinegar
Sugar or honey

Pit and crush or chop the fruit well; combine with 1 cup vinegar for every pound of fruit and steep in a tightly closed container in a cool spot for at least 2 weeks. For a stronger fruit flavor, repeat the procedure with a fresh batch of crushed fruit, steeping for another 2 to 3 weeks.

Strain the flavored vinegar (or the reserved cherry vinegar from the pickled cherries) into a nonreactive saucepan and add sugar or honey to taste. Bring the mixture to a simmer over medium heat and cook, uncovered, for 3 minutes. Cool the vinegar and skim off any foam. Strain into completely dry, sterilized bottles; cap, label, and store in a cool dark place.

Variations: Try peaches, pears, apricots, cranberries, strawberries, raspberries, or a mixture of fruits.

INFUSED LIQUORS

Infused liquors are simple to prepare but require excellent ingredients. Don't expect finesse in your finished product if you start with cheap spirits; choose quality, but by no means do you need to use "top shelf" or premium brands. Begin with a base of brandy, vodka, gin, or grain alcohol—wine, beer, and fortified wines are not sufficiently strong enough to prevent spoilage. Fruits, herbs, and spices must be fully ripe and flavorful and impeccably fresh and clean for a superior result. Marry the fruit with the character of the spirit or choose an unflavored eau de vie (pure grain alcohol) to let the unadulterated fruit flavor shine on its own. It is important to steep and bottle your spirit infusions in nonreactive ceramic or glass containers, as metal or plastic may impart off flavors. Sweetening buffers the harshness of some spirits as well as dilutes the finished alcohol content.

Fun fact: Fruit-steeped spirits flavored with spices and honey or sugar were often served to mark the ratification of an agreement between parties in a celebratory toast and thus came to be called *ratafia*.

RASPBERRY CORDIAL

· ·

A warming nip of summer for a cold winter's night—sip neat or add a splash to a flute of champagne for a twist on a traditional Kir cocktail.

Season: Mid- to late summer

Yield: About 4 to 5 cups

Store: Cool, dark pantry

· ·

4 cups fresh raspberries, picked over, rinsed, and drained

1 quart vodka

Simple syrup to taste (see page 90)

Put the berries in a bowl and crush to a coarse purée. Transfer the berries to a 2-quart glass jar and fill to the very top with vodka; exposure to air during steeping may cause fermentation and spoilage. Seal the jar and place out of direct light to steep for 8 to 10 weeks, gently agitating the jar and its contents several times a week.

When you are satisfied with the fruity strength of the flavor, strain the infusion through a sieve lined with dampened cheesecloth into a bowl. Discard the berries. Add ¼ to 1 cup simple syrup, depending on whether the finished liquor is meant to be blended with other mixers or sipped neat; adjust to taste.

Using a funnel, pour the cordial into clean, dry bottles and securely cork or seal to prevent evaporation. Store in a cool dark place; age for at least 4 to 6 weeks to allow the cordial to mature and mellow.

Variations: Add the zest of an organic lemon or ½ vanilla bean, split lengthwise, to the berries when steeping.

SIMPLE SYRUP

"Simply" sugar dissolved in water, this syrup is perfect for sweetening many kitchen preparations such as fruit salad as well as iced tea and other beverages.

2 cups white sugar

1 cup water

Bring the sugar and water to a boil in a small saucepan. Reduce heat and stir until the sugar is completely dissolved. Cool to room temperature, seal in an airtight container, and store in the refrigerator for up to 6 months.

HOMEMADE FROZEN JUICE CONCENTRATE

Use the following recipe when you have an abundance of fresh juice—think apple cider in the fall or citrus when it is fresh, plentiful, and low-priced during the winter. Beyond being an efficient way to store juice, there are many other delicious ways you can use these juice concentrates. Marinades, sauces, and even ice creams are easily started from these intensely flavored condensed bases.

> **Season: Summer through fall**
> **Yield: Variable**
> **Store: Freezer (1 year; citrus, 4 to 6 months)**

Any quantity fresh fruit juice

Pour fruit juice into a large, narrow-necked container, such as a plastic gallon jug or a clean wine bottle, filling the container no more than ¾ full to allow for expansion; cap and freeze. Once frozen, remove the cap and invert the jug or bottle, suspended by its "shoulders," over a wide mouth jar to collect the concentrated juice drips. The juicier bits melt before the plain water crystals and drain into the jar below. When the drips running off are no longer sweet and colored, remove the jug. Finish melting the ice and discard the now plain water. Repeat this freezing and dripping procedure two more times (three times total) to attain a fine concentrate. Bottle or package in rigid containers and store in the freezer.

Note: Don't try to rush the draining process with heat, which will melt the plain water crystals and dilute the finished juice concentrate.

FRUIT LEATHER

This is a resourceful and tasty way to make use of overly ripe fruit that wouldn't be suitable for other forms of preserving. The concentrated sugars and chewy texture of these "fruit rolls" are a favorite of young children (although perhaps not of their dentists). A food processor will create a smooth purée; a food mill will do a better job of removing tiny seeds that can create a disagreeably grainy final product.

Season: Summer through fall
Yield: Depends on your starting quantity of fruit
Store: Cool, dark pantry (6 months)

Fruit, fresh or cooked
Water or fruit juice
Lemon juice

Peel, pit, and purée whichever fruit or combination of fruits you intend to make into leather. Add a small amount of liquid (juice or water) to attain a pourable consistency. Add a dash of lemon juice to raw fruits to prevent browning; cooked fruits retain their vibrant color when dried.

Line a drying tray or sheet pan with plastic wrap or use nonstick silicon sheets. Lightly spray with vegetable oil.

Pour the purée onto the prepared surface and spread to an equal thickness by carefully tilting the pan or tray one way and then another. A thin, even layer will dry the quickest; 2 to 2¼ cups purée will spread to the recommended ⅛ to ¼ inch depth on a standard-sized sheet pan.

Place your prepared trays out in the sun or into a dehydrator. When drying fruit leather in an oven, keep the temperature low—120 to 130°F—and air circulation high to avoid scorching.

When the top side is dry (anywhere from 6 to 8 hours), invert the leather onto another lined or oiled pan, peel off the first lining, and continue to dry for another 6 to 8 hours until completely dry but not brittle.

Cool the finished fruit leather on a wire rack. Cut into wide strips and dust with cornstarch to prevent sticking, then roll into tubes. Store the finished rolls, wrapped in plastic, in an airtight container.

CRANBERRY "RAISINS"

Candied cranberries, with their mouth puckering, sweet-tart flavor and deep ruby color, are a wonderful addition to granola, baked goods, and savory meats. Make this recipe when fresh berries first appear in markets in the fall and you'll be ready for holiday feasts and gifting.

Season: Fall
Yield: 1 to 1 1/2 cups (may be multiplied)
Store: Cool, dark pantry

1 1/2 cups fresh cranberries, picked over, rinsed, and drained
1 1/2 cups sugar
1 1/4 cups water

Prick each berry with a needle. Combine the sugar and water in a sauté pan and bring to 230°F, stirring to dissolve the sugar. Add the cranberries and gently simmer until the syrup passes the jelly test (see page 76); the berries will burst, but that will not affect the finished product.

Lightly oil sheet pans or dehydrator trays and line with baking parchment. Strain the berries and spread in the pans. Separate the individual berries with your fingers or two small forks as they cool. Dry in a low oven or electric dehydrator until no longer tacky. Dried cranberries may be rolled in more sugar to keep them from sticking together. Store at room temperature in a tightly closed container.

Variations: To candy citrus peel, remove rind from citrus (lemon, orange, lime, grapefruit) and scrape with a spoon to remove the bitter white pith. Cut the rind into ¼-inch strips and cover with water in a small saucepan. Bring to a boil and simmer, uncovered, for 30 minutes. Drain, cover with more water, and repeat the boiling process. Drain the peel and proceed as for the candied cranberries.

To candy ginger, substitute ⅛-inch sliced "coins" of peeled fresh ginger for cranberries, simmering in the sugar syrup for 45 minutes or until the ginger is completely tender. Drain, reserving the now richly flavored syrup for other uses, and proceed with drying and sugaring.

SPICED LEMONS IN OIL

Serve these supple cured lemons with hors d'oeuvres, minced in salads, or as an accompaniment to grilled fish. The flavored oil may be used in vinaigrettes and marinades.

Season: Any time
Yield: 2 cups
Store: Refrigerator (6 months)

2 lemons, preferably organic
½ cup freshly squeezed lemon juice
⅓ cup kosher salt
16 whole cloves
1 3-inch cinnamon stick
½ teaspoon black peppercorns
Olive oil

Scrub each lemon well to thoroughly clean. Slice lengthwise into 8 wedges and toss with the lemon juice and salt in a bowl. Stud the peel of each wedge with 2 cloves and pack the fruit and the remaining spices into a 2-cup glass jar with a nonmetal lid; pour any remaining juices into the jar. Seal or cork the jar and allow the lemons to ripen at room temperature for 7 days. Shake daily to distribute the salt, spices, and juices. Add olive oil to top the jar and age for 3 to 4 weeks before using. Store in the refrigerator for up to 6 months.

Variation: Substitute fresh limes for the lemons.

VEGETABLES

Most cuisines throughout the world have a long tradition of pickles, chutneys, and other tasty side dishes. These preserved foods and condiments complement everyday meals as well as holiday feasts, from the exotic flavors of the Middle East and Asia to the seven sweets and seven sours, traditional fare of the Pennsylvania Dutch.

OLD-FASHIONED CROCK PICKLES

Crock pickles cure in a saltwater solution by means of fermentation caused by lactic acid bacteria, a cloudy film or scum that floats on the surface of the brine. Naturally, in this day and age of sanitation and concern about harmful microorganisms, this scum appears somewhat suspect. In fact, lactic acid is responsible for changing the pickles from bright green to an olive or yellow green and produces the characteristically tart, sour flavor we associate with pickles.

For every 5 pounds of cucumbers you will need one gallon of pickling capacity; for example, a 5-gallon crock will hold 25 pounds of cucumbers. Select a ceramic crock, large glass jar, or food-grade plastic container; do not use a metal pot, as it will negatively react with the vinegar.

Season: Mid- to late summer

Yield: 4 quarts

Store: Cool, dark pantry

For every gallon of finished pickles you'll need:

- 4 to 5 pounds clean, unwaxed, firm cucumbers about
    4 to 6 inches long
- 2 tablespoons dill seed or 4 to 5 heads fresh dill weed
- 2 cloves garlic
- 2 dried red peppers
- 8 cups water
- ½ cup pickling salt
- ¼ cup vinegar
- 2 teaspoons whole mixed pickling spices (see page 102)

Carefully pick through the cucumbers and discard any that are bruised or have soft spots; wash well. Place half of the dill, 1 clove garlic, and 1 pepper at the bottom of your clean crock. Add the cucumbers and the remaining dill, garlic, and pepper.

Bring the water, salt, vinegar, and pickling spice to a boil over medium-high heat. Cover and simmer for 5 minutes. Remove from heat and allow this brine to cool *completely* before pouring over the cucumbers in the crock. Weight a dinner plate or a glass pie plate with a heavy-duty, food-grade plastic bag filled with water and place in the crock to keep the fermenting pickles at least 2 inches below the surface of the brine.

Store the crock of cucumbers at room temperature; fermentation will take longer to complete under cool temperatures, whereas excessively warm temperatures will result in soft pickles. Check the crock daily and skim any scum that appears. A clean cloth draped over the crock will keep out dust and other contaminants. Complete fermentation for "full sours" will take about 3 weeks; however, you can remove pickles from their brine before that if you prefer what are known as kosher-style or half-sours.

Fully fermented pickles covered with brine may be refrigerated in jars for months or canned for stable shelf storage. To can the pickles, pour the brine into a pan, heat slowly to a boil, and simmer for 5 minutes. Fill hot sterile pint or quart jars with pickles and top with hot brine, leaving ½ inch headspace. Brine may be strained through a clean cloth or paper coffee filter to reduce cloudiness, if desired. Place lids on the filled jars and process in a water bath (page 34): pints for 15 minutes, quarts for 20 minutes.

SAUERKRAUT

A practical nineteenth century doctor remarked "Cabbage is the physician of the poor." Indeed, sauerkraut, or fermented cabbage, is an aid to digestion, promotes health, and is a lasting, delicious, low-calorie vegetable to keep on hand in the refrigerator.

Season: Summer through fall
Yield: About 2 quarts
Store: Refrigerator, canned or frozen

5 pounds firm white cabbage, quartered, cored, and finely shredded
3 tablespoons pickling salt

Combine the cabbage and salt in a large bowl and mix thoroughly with scrupulously clean hands or a spoon; you don't want to introduce bad bacteria to the fermentation process. Let stand for about 15 minutes to allow the cabbage to soften and begin to release its juices.

Layer the cabbage into a gallon crock or jar, firmly tamping down each addition to bring juices to the surface. Fill to within 4 to 5 inches of the top of the container and add any remaining juices from the bowl.

Fill a heavy-duty, food-grade plastic bag with water and place it on the cabbage to seal out the air and provide a weight to keep the fermenting cabbage submerged in its juices. Cover the crock or jar with a clean cloth and store at room temperature (70 to 75°F).

Fermentation will cause the mixture to bubble and froth. Check the crock a couple of times a week and skim any scum that appears. Fermentation is complete when all bubbling stops, generally 3 to 4 weeks. At cooler temperatures (60°F), fermentation can take up to 5 to 6 weeks.

Pack the fully fermented sauerkraut into clean glass jars; if your jars have metal lids, first line them with plastic wrap or waxed paper before capping. Kraut will store in the refrigerator for months. Freeze or can for long-term storage. To can, bring the sauerkraut and its liquid to a boil and fill hot, sterilized pint or quart jars. Follow water-bath canning instructions (page 34) and process pints for 10 minutes, quarts for 15 minutes.

Variations: Add whole caraway seed or juniper berries to the salted cabbage for additional flavor. This same fermenting process may be applied to any finely shredded or thinly sliced vegetable. Try carrots, beans, green tomatoes, root vegetables, and hearty greens, adding garlic, celery, coriander, and onion for interesting flavor blends.

MIXED PICKLING SPICES

Combine:

    1 tablespoon yellow mustard seed

    2 tablespoons whole allspice

    2 tablespoons whole coriander

    2 teaspoons black peppercorns

    2 dried bay leaves, crumbled

    2 dried red chili peppers, crumbled

Store the mixture in an airtight container in a cool, dark pantry. May be used in any pickle recipe.

PICKLING WITH VINEGAR

It is important to carefully follow pickling recipe instructions based on vinegar to maintain proper acidity for safe shelf storage. If you find the finished pickles to be too sour or tart, add a small amount of sugar to the recipe to buffer, but do not reduce or dilute the amount of vinegar called for in the recipe. Finished pickles may be refrigerated for short-term storage or canned in a hot water bath for long-term storage.

PICKLING SECRETS

- Always start with clean, fresh, unblemished ingredients.

- Wash food well but do not soak; any water that has been absorbed will later dilute the pickling solution and throw off the acidity balance.

- Never use zinc, copper, brass, galvanized metal, or iron containers or utensils; these will react with the vinegar. Plastic containers must be food-grade.

- Use pure granulated pickling salt or other fine, noniodized table salt.

- Use whole, fresh herbs and spices for the best flavor.

- Use white or brown sugar or honey to sweeten pickles; however, brown sugar will darken the final product, and honey will alter the finished flavor.

- If your water is heavily chlorinated or especially hard, use bottled water to avoid a cloudy brine and off-colors in the finished product.

GARLIC DILL PICKLES

· ·

Season: Mid- to late summer
Yield: 6 to 7 pints
Store: Cool, dark pantry

· ·

4 pounds pickling cucumbers, about 4 inches long, scrubbed and
    cut in half lengthwise
14 cloves garlic, split in half (28 halves)
¼ cup pickling or other fine, noniodized salt
2¾ cups cider vinegar
3 cups water
14 heads fresh dill weed
28 peppercorns

Heat the garlic, salt, vinegar, and water to boiling. Remove the garlic
and place 4 halves in each hot, sterilized jar (if the cucumbers fill only 6
jars, add the remaining halves to 4 of the jars). Pack the cucumbers into
the jars and divide the dill and peppercorns evenly among them.

    Pour the hot vinegar solution over the cucumbers, allowing ½ inch
headspace. Adjust the lids. Follow water-bath canning instructions
(page 34) and process for 10 minutes. Store for at least 6 weeks before
serving.

BREAD-AND-BUTTER PICKLES

Season: Mid- to late summer
Yield: 7 to 9 pints
Store: Cool, dark pantry

6 pounds pickling cucumbers, cut into 1/8-inch slices
1/2 cup pickling or other fine noniodized salt
Crushed ice
4 cups cider vinegar
4 cups sugar
2 teaspoons celery seed
1 tablespoon whole allspice
2 tablespoons mustard seed

Combine the cucumbers and salt in a mixing bowl and mix. Completely cover with the ice and let stand for 3 to 4 hours. Drain thoroughly, picking out any remaining unmelted ice.

Bring the vinegar, sugar, celery seed, allspice, and mustard seed to a boil in an 8-quart saucepan, stirring to dissolve the sugar. Simmer uncovered for 5 minutes. Add the cucumber slices to the vinegar syrup and return to a simmer; stir gently to make sure heat is evenly distributed throughout the mixture.

Carefully ladle the pickles into hot, sterilized jars, allowing 1/2 inch headspace. Follow water-bath canning instructions (page 34) and process for 10 minutes. Store for a least a month and then refrigerate before serving.

Variation: For traditional bread-and-butter pickles with onions, add 1 cup peeled and thinly sliced small white onions along with the cucumbers to the vinegar syrup and proceed with instructions.

QUICK PICKLES

Crisp, tangy, and ready in only a couple of hours—nearly instant picnic food, and a wonderful accompaniment to pulled pork barbecue.

Season: Any time
Yield: 4 quarts
Store: Refrigerator (2 weeks)

2 bunches whole radishes, tops removed

6 whole shallots, peeled

Several sprigs fresh thyme

3 to 4 carrots, peeled and sliced lengthwise into sticks

2 Green, red, orange, and/or yellow bell peppers, sliced

1 jalapeño pepper, halved

1 fresh bay leaf

½ pound green beans

½ knob fresh fennel, sliced

Several sprigs fresh chervil or tarragon

1 large cucumber, cut into ¼ inch slices

½ medium red onion, sliced

2 sprigs dill

6 cups white wine vinegar

1¼ cups sugar

2 tablespoons kosher salt

2 teaspoons black peppercorns

Thoroughly wash and dry 4 quart jars and their lids in hot soapy water.

Bring a small saucepan of water to a boil. Meanwhile, fill a mixing bowl with ice and cold water. Add the shallots to the boiling water and cook just until tender. Leave the water boiling; remove the shallots with a slotted spoon and transfer to the ice water bath to cool. Drain and set aside. Add the radishes to the boiling water and blanch for 30 seconds; transfer to the ice water bath to cool. Drain.

Pack the jars as follows:

- Shallots, radishes, and thyme
- Carrots, sweet and hot pepper, and bay leaf
- Beans, fennel, and chervil or tarragon
- Cucumber, red onion, and dill

In a large nonreactive saucepan combine the vinegar, sugar, salt, peppercorns, and ½ cup water. Bring to a boil, stirring to dissolve the sugar and salt. Remove from heat. Pour the hot marinade over the vegetables in each jar to cover. Secure the lids and let cool to room temperature. May be served at once or stored in the refrigerator.

AND MORE

A chutney or ketchup is a concoction prepared with fruit, vegetables, or combination of the two, and salt, vinegar, spices, and sugar. Both are cooked and processed much like a jam; however, chutney retains a chunky texture, whereas ketchup is puréed and strained for a smooth, pourable consistency.

PICKLED EGGPLANT CHUTNEY

This spicy condiment is delicious with curries or served with sharp cheese and pickles for a British ploughman's lunch. Adjust the quantity of peppers to your desired heat level.

Season: Late summer through fall
Yield: 3 pints
Store: Cool, dark pantry

2 large eggplants, unpeeled
3 tablespoons distilled white vinegar
2 cloves garlic, minced
2 tablespoons prepared chili powder
2 teaspoons ground ginger
2 teaspoons turmeric
1 tablespoon cumin seed
1 tablespoon fenugreek seed
⅓ cup vegetable oil
1¼ cups distilled white vinegar
1 cup sugar
2 to 4 hot red chilies, seeded and finely chopped
⅓ cup grated fresh ginger
2 tablespoons pickling salt

Cut the eggplant into small cubes and reserve.

Combine the vinegar, garlic, chili powder, ground ginger, and turmeric in a small bowl to form a paste; reserve.

In a large saucepan, heat the oil over medium high heat and briefly sauté the cumin and fenugreek seed. Add the eggplant and cook until tender, about 10 minutes. Reduce heat and add the reserved spice paste and the vinegar, sugar, chili peppers, fresh ginger, and pickling salt. Bring to a boil and stir for 5 minutes.

Ladle the chutney into hot, sterilized half-pint or pint jars, allowing ½ inch headspace. Follow water-bath canning instructions (page 34) and process for 15 minutes for half-pints, 20 minutes for pints.

APPLE CRANBERRY KETCHUP

This sweet, tart relish is as delicious with a holiday turkey as with barbe-cued burgers in summer.

Season: Fall

Yield: 3 pints

Store: Cool, dark pantry

1½ cups finely chopped mild onion

4 strips orange zest, 1 inch wide, scraped to remove bitter
   white pith

4 cups water

4 cups cranberries, fresh or frozen (thawed)

6 tart apples, peeled, cored, and quartered

2 cups cider vinegar

1 cup packed brown sugar, or more if desired

2 teaspoons pickling salt

1 teaspoon mustard powder

¼ teaspoon ground cloves

1 teaspoon ground ginger

1½ teaspoons ground cinnamon

Bring the onion, orange zest, and water to a boil in a preserving pan. Cover and simmer for 10 minutes or until the onions are tender and translucent.

Add the cranberries and apples to the onions and bring the mixture to a boil; partially cover and simmer until the fruit is very soft, about 15 minutes. Empty everything into a bowl to cool slightly.

Working with half the mixture at a time, whirl in a food processor or blender until very finely puréed; transfer the purée into the rinsed-out preserving pan. Optional: for a very smooth texture, press the purée through a fine sieve before returning to the pan.

Add the vinegar, brown sugar, salt, mustard, cloves, ginger, and cinnamon and bring to a boil over medium heat, stirring constantly to prevent the ketchup from scorching. Cook until thickened to your desired consistency. Carefully ladle the hot ketchup into hot, sterilized pint jars, allowing ¼ inch headspace. Follow water-bath canning instructions (page 34) and process for 15 minutes. The ketchup is ready for serving in a few days, but the flavors will continue to mellow for several weeks.

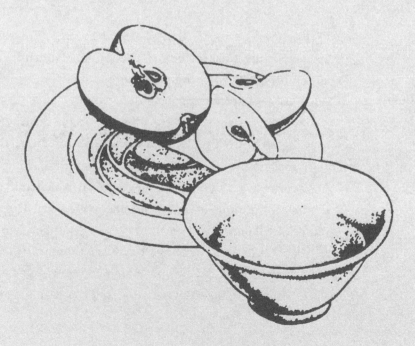

OVEN-DRIED TOMATOES

Small jars of dried tomatoes packed in oil are costly deli items. Preparing your own when the summer crop is abundant is easy and every bit as tasty.

Season: Late summer through fall

Yield: 1 pint

Store: Refrigerator or cool, dark pantry

4 pounds ripe but not overly soft Italian paste-type
   (plum, Roma) tomatoes
Salt
White vinegar
1 sprig fresh rosemary
Olive oil

Preheat oven to 200°F. Line sheet pans with foil or parchment paper and set cooling racks on them. Halve the small tomatoes and quarter the larger ones, removing the tough core at the stem end. Gently squeeze the tomatoes to remove most of the seeds.

Arrange the tomatoes, cut sides up, on the cooling racks. Sprinkle them lightly with salt. Place pans in the oven and prop the door open to allow moisture to escape; a convection oven with a built-in fan is ideal. The tomatoes are done when they have shriveled and are leathery but not brittle. Their color should be a deep ruby red. The amount of time required will depend on the tomatoes, but count on 6 to 8 hours.

Cool the tomatoes completely. Place them in a bowl and sprinkle with vinegar, tossing with your hands to lightly moisten them. With a slotted spoon, remove the tomatoes and drain on paper toweling, patting them to thoroughly dry.

Pack the tomatoes into a sterilized pint jar together with the rose-mary. Pour in enough olive oil to completely cover the tomatoes and cap securely. Store at cool room temperature for 1 month before serving. Refrigerate after opening.

DRIED SWEET CORN

Before the advent of freezers, resourceful Midwesterners routinely dried their sweet corn harvest to hold it through the winter. This recipe is an enriched variation on that old-time practice.

Season: Late summer through fall
Yield: 2 quarts
Store: Cool, dark pantry

16 cups fresh sweet corn, cut from the cob (about 32 ears!)
1½ tablespoons salt
1 to 6 tablespoons sugar, depending on the sweetness of
    your corn to begin with
½ cup heavy cream

Combine all the ingredients in a preserving pan and cook over low heat, stirring constantly to prevent scorching, until the cream has been completely absorbed.

Divide the corn between two large sheet pans, spreading it to a roughly even, 2-kernel depth. Dry in a warm oven (200°F) with the door propped open to allow moisture to escape; a convection oven with a built-in fan is ideal, or you could use an electric dehydrator. Stir the corn frequently as it dries. It's done when it has shriveled and is golden and quite crisp. Depending on your oven, the corn—even the weather—this will take anywhere from 4 to 6 hours.

Cool the corn completely before packaging it in airtight containers. Check the containers in a couple of days; if there is any sign of moisture on the inside of the jars, return the corn to the oven for further drying.

SPRING TONIC NETTLE PURÉE

In early spring, stinging nettles emerge in weed lots and woodlands. Rich in vitamins and minerals, nettles are a nutritional powerhouse and well worth a little cautious foraging (see below). There is only a brief window of time when the tender new growth can be harvested. Be sure to freeze plenty of this purée for luscious, velvety soup or a rich sauce for fish or poultry.

Season: Spring
Yield: Variable
Store: Freezer (6 months)

They don't call them stinging nettles for nothing! Until the greens have been blanched or cooked in some way, the tiny hairs that cover the plants cause a very painful irritation. When gathering nettles, protect yourself with long pants, long sleeves, and sturdy garden gloves. Using a pair of scissors, snip the top 6 to 8 inches of tender spring growth, letting it drop directly into a paper bag.

Back in the kitchen, using tongs, swish the nettles in cool water to remove grit; snip the leaves from the tougher stems. Bring a pot of salted water to a boil; again using tongs to protect yourself, drop the nettle leaves into the boiling water and cook for 2 minutes. Using a slotted spoon, remove the blanched leaves and plunge into a large bowl of cool water. Gather the leaves into a bunch and with your hands squeeze out as much water as you can—the cooking disables the sting. Package in airtight containers or zip-locking bags and freeze as you would other blanched greens (see page 20).

Variation: At its best in early spring, sorrel—a tart, lemony garden green—can be processed in the same way.

POTTED MUSHROOMS

This rich, pungent spread relies on both fresh and dried mushrooms for its depth of flavor. Make this in the fall when farmers markets are rich with different varieties of wild mushrooms; choose an assortment of button, chanterelle, porcini, and hedgehog. Smear on thin crackers or croutons for a canapé, swirl into hot pasta, or top grilled meats.

Season: Fall
Yield: 3 to 4 cups
Store: Refrigerator (3 weeks)

1 ounce dried porcini mushrooms

⅔ cup warm water

2 tablespoons sherry

2 shallots, peeled and sliced

1 clove garlic, peeled and sliced

½ teaspoon salt

¼ teaspoon freshly ground nutmeg

Large pinch of dried thyme

Small piece of dried bay leaf (about ½ inch square)

Tiny pinch of ground cloves

¾ pound fresh, firm cultivated and wild mushrooms, stems removed

Freshly ground black pepper

½ cup butter, cut into ¼-inch slices

½ to ¾ cup clarified butter (see page 147)

Soak the dried mushrooms in warm water for several hours or overnight until very soft.

Preheat oven to 300°F. With a slotted spoon, lift the mushrooms out of the liquid and put them into the bowl of a food processor; let the soaking liquid settle, then pour it into the food processor, leaving any grit or sand behind. Add the sherry, shallots, garlic, salt, nutmeg, thyme, bay leaf, and cloves and process the mixture to a fine purée. Scrape the purée into a bowl and reserve.

Working in batches if necessary, process the fresh mushrooms in the food processor until very finely chopped. Add the reserved purée and blend everything together. Scrape this mixture into an ovenproof 3-cup dish and set it into a slightly larger baking pan. Cover the inner dish tightly with foil and add a metal lid or ovenproof plate to hold it in place. Pour enough boiling water into the outer pan to come up to an inch below the rim of the inner dish.

Bake the mushroom mixture, adding more water as necessary to maintain the proper level, for 1½ hours. Stir the mushrooms, replace the foil, and return to the oven for another hour for a total of 2½ hours. The mushrooms should be very tender, with an almost jelly-like texture. Remove the foil and continue baking, uncovered, for an additional ½ hour. Remove from oven and set the inner dish on a rack to cool to lukewarm.

Taste the potted mushrooms and add pepper to taste, balancing any other seasonings as you see fit; the flavor will be quite strong. Add the butter slices, one-third at a time, whisking well after each addition until the butter is fully incorporated into the mushroom mixture. Taste for final seasoning.

Pack the potted mushrooms into two or three serving crocks or ramekins and smooth the tops; chill, uncovered, until the mixture sets firmly. Melt the clarified butter and pour a layer about ¼ inch thick over the chilled mushrooms, being sure to cover the entire surface and taking care to seal the butter layer to the sides of the container. Cover and refrigerate. Before serving, allow the potted mushrooms to soften slightly at room temperature. Leftovers should be used within a few days.

ROASTED PEPPERS AND EGGPLANT IN GARLIC OIL

A jar of this and you're set for an instant antipasto dish with a rich, smoky flavor; choose a colorful mix of red, orange, and yellow peppers, and combine hot and sweet peppers for an added kick.

Season: Late summer through fall
Yield: 2 pints
Store: Cool, dark pantry or freezer

5 small Japanese eggplants, cut into $\frac{1}{2}$-inch-thick slices

6 to 7 sweet bell or hot peppers

1 cup olive oil

3 cloves garlic, peeled and sliced

$\frac{1}{4}$ teaspoon hot pepper flakes (omit if you are using a mix of hot and sweet peppers)

$\frac{1}{2}$ teaspoon pickling salt

$\frac{3}{4}$ cup cider vinegar

Preheat the broiler. Broil the eggplants on a greased sheet pan about 4 inches from the heat, turning once, until they are lightly browned, about 15 minutes.

Broil or roast the whole peppers until their skins are completely blackened; place in a paper bag to steam for 10 minutes. When cool, peel off the charred skin, quarter, and remove the seeds.

Heat the olive oil, garlic, hot pepper flakes, salt, and vinegar and simmer for 5 minutes. Layer the eggplant slices and pepper quarters into hot, sterilized pint jars. Top off with the hot seasoned oil, allowing $\frac{1}{2}$ inch headspace.

To can: seal jars and follow water-bath canning instructions (page 34) and process for 15 minutes. Allow flavors to blend for 2 weeks before serving.

To freeze: seal jars and allow to cool completely before freezing. Thaw peppers slowly in the refrigerator before serving.

Variation: This recipe may be prepared with just peppers or just eggplant.

MEAT, FISH, AND DAIRY

Pastured meat, wild fish, and dairy products free from pesticides and antibiotics are good for our health and that of the planet as well. Tended with traditional and sustainable practices that put less of a burden on our environment, the resulting foods are remarkably flavorful, with vivid color and maximum nutritional value. We fish the river or boat the waters from which we pull salmon or bass and become even more aware of the responsibility to preserve habitat and our place within a global ecosystem. Whether your eggs come from the backyard coop or the farmers market, your bacon from the butcher or the co-op, choosing wholesome meat, fish, and dairy foods does make a difference.

CURING MEAT AT HOME

Some cured meat recipes call for the addition of a curing salt. Sodium nitrite, sometimes referred to as pink salt, is an important component of air-dried sausages and cold smoking. In these processes, the meat is held for a protracted period at 40 to 140°F—temperatures at which dangerous bacteria can quickly multiply. Nitrites kill a range of dangerous bacteria and help preserve the pink flesh we associate with clean healthy meat as well as lend a characteristic "cured" flavor to the end product. Nitrites remain controversial because of their connection with nitrosamine, a cancer-causing compound. Recipes that are cooked, like confit, or prepared under refrigeration, like corned beef or gravlax, do not require the addition of nitrites for food safety, although they will not have the rosy hue and cured flavor associated with curing salts.

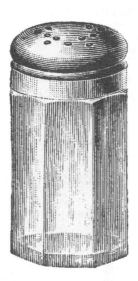

BEEF JERKY

Free from the additives and preservatives present in commercial products, homemade beef jerky is a healthy and nutritious snack. Adjust the following recipe to your preference for spiciness. Note: the more heavily the jerky is seasoned and the more thoroughly it is dried, the better it will keep.

Season: Any time
Yield: About ¾ pound
Store: Refrigerator or freezer

3 pounds lean beef (flank or round steak)
1½ tablespoons kosher salt
¼ cup brown sugar, lightly packed
1 teaspoon black pepper, crushed

To facilitate cutting the thinnest slices, which will in turn dry the quickest, freeze the beef, uncovered, for 1 to 2 hours, just until ice crystals form. Trim all fat off the meat and slice with the grain of the muscle into strips, 1 inch wide by ⅛ to ¼ inch thick.

Combine the salt, brown sugar, and pepper in a bowl; add the meat strips and mix well. Cover and refrigerate for 12 to 24 hours.

Remove the meat from the cure and pat dry. Place the strips on dryer trays if using a dehydrator or on a wire rack set over a sheet pan for oven drying. Dry at 100 to 140°F until the jerky is completely dry to the touch, dark, and just slightly flexible. Drying time will vary with heat source and air circulation; estimate 6 to 10 hours and monitor closely.

Cool completely and store in an airtight container. Store in the refrigerator for a few months or freeze for long-term storage.

Variation: Garlic powder, onion powder, hot pepper sauce, dry mustard powder, Worcestershire sauce, and soy sauce may be added to boost the spiciness.

BASIC 10-PERCENT BRINE

Combine 1½ to 2 cups kosher salt and ½ cup sugar in 1 gallon of water in a large stockpot over medium heat. Fresh herbs, spices, and aromatic vegetables are often added for extra flavor. Bring ingredients to a simmer and stir until sugar and salt are completely dissolved. If you are brining meat or fish, cool completely before proceeding. To reduce chilling time, heat the salt, sugar, and any other ingredients in half the amount of required water. Once everything is dissolved, add the remaining water, either cold or as ice water. Test: A 10-percent brine will float a 2-ounce (Large) egg to the surface of the liquid; adjust the salt as necessary.

CORNED BEEF

• •

Cured in a brine, corned beef is easy to prepare at home and doesn't require special equipment, merely space in the refrigerator. Although the following recipe involves beef, you can also "pickle" pork, poultry, and various other meats in this fashion. Note: When salting or brining, use only glass, glazed stoneware, or other nonmetallic containers to prevent a nasty, corrosive interaction with the food.

Season: Any time
Yield: 5 pounds
Store: Freezer

• •

1 gallon water
2 cups kosher salt
½ cup sugar
3 garlic cloves, minced
2 tablespoons pickling spice (see page 102)
5 pounds beef brisket

Prepare a brine with the water, salt, sugar, garlic, and spices (see Basic 10-Percent Brine on page 124) and chill completely before proceeding with the recipe.

Place the brisket in the brine weighted down with a dinner plate or a glass pie plate or a heavy-duty, food-grade plastic bag filled with water to keep it completely submerged. Refrigerate, turning the meat every day or so, for 5 days to 2 weeks, depending on how strong you prefer the finished cure.

At the end of the curing time, remove the brisket from the brine and rinse thoroughly under cool, running water. Follow a recipe to prepare corned beef, or wrap it in several layers of heavy butcher paper and store under refrigeration for up to one week; properly wrapped corned beef may be frozen for one month (see page 24).

Variation: Hot red pepper flakes, coriander, juniper berries, and other aromatics may be added to the brine for added flavor. Smoking the cured corned beef will produce pastrami, a deli favorite.

GRAVLAX

Salmon preserved in a salt and sugar cure is a culinary tradition in many parts of the world. In Scandinavia, dill and other seasonings are added to the cure to produce gravlax, which is served with crisp crackers or black bread as part of a traditional smorgasbord. Pacific Northwest and Alaskan Native Americans often cured their catch in this manner, later smoking it over a fire to build their food stores. Today, these cures are largely employed for the flavors they impart and to transform the flesh to a buttery, tender texture. To avoid wasting your efforts, cure only what you plan to serve within a week's time. Finished gravlax may be frozen for up to a month; however, the texture will be affected.

   Note. Fresh caught fish may contain dangerous parasites; because this process does not involve cooking, for safety's sake it is recommended that you start with commercially frozen fish or freeze the finished cured salmon for 7 days at −10°F. Use a meticulously clean plastic cutting board. There is much discussion as to whether or not to press the fish with a weighted plate or pie pan during the curing process; doing so may speed the cure by helping to extract the juices, however the final product will be more dense, and less moist.

Season: Any time
Yield: Variable
Store: Refrigerator (2 weeks)

Filet of salmon, thawed (see above)
1 cup salt
2 cups sugar
Fresh dill weed, finely chopped

Rinse the salmon and lay it on a clean plastic cutting board. Check for pin bones along the spine by gently massaging the flesh; remove the tiny bones with tweezers or needle-nose pliers.

Combine the salt and sugar in a bowl. Depending on the amount of fish you are curing, you may not need the full amount; store any extra cure in a clearly labeled zip-locking bag.

If you are working with an entire filet, cut it in half; smaller sections of the filet may be left whole. Place the salmon, skin side down, on a sheet of plastic wrap. Coat the flesh with the salt-sugar mix and top with a generous handful of dill to heavily smother the fish. For larger portions, sandwich the dill between the two half filets. Wrap the fish-cure-herb package tightly in another layer of plastic wrap and place in a baking dish to catch the juices that will begin to exude.

Allow the fish to stand at room temperature until the sugar and salt cure have melted into the flesh—no more than 6 hours. Place the fish—still in the baking dish—in the refrigerator for 2 to 3 days depending on how strong a cure you are after. Turn the fish package once a day.

The flesh will turn a brilliant orange and firm up as it loses moisture, absorbing the flavors of the seasonings in the process. To serve, rinse the salmon and dry thoroughly. Slice thinly on the bias and remove the skin. Crème fraîche or sour cream, lemon wedges, capers, and freshly ground pepper are traditional accompaniments.

Variations: Substitute fresh fennel fronds for the dill weed and sprinkle lightly with Pernod, an anise-flavored liquor, along with the salt and sugar. Citrus juices, bay leaf, and other seasonings may also be substituted for a different flavor profile. In any case, the process and curing remains the same.

ODE TO FAT

The French refer to rich meats—such as pork, duck, goose, and rabbit—cooked and preserved in fat as a *confit*, which literally translates as "to preserve." In other recipes in this section, economical cuts of meat are gently cooked in fat and wine or broth and aromatic seasonings until meltingly tender, then shredded or processed to a coarse paste—*rillettes*, to the French. Poached fish or shellfish, being less fatty and more delicately flavored, may be prepared in a similar manner, using butter to preserve.

In each instance, fat forms a protective seal to keep air and bacteria out of the finished preserves. At one time a kitchen art born of necessity to create lasting food stores, today these preparations are all about infusing flavor and richness. As Michael Ruhlman states in his great book *Charcuterie: The Craft of Salting, Smoking, and Curing*, "Having solved the survival issue, we have the luxury to think about pleasure, about refinement."

These deliciously unctuous preparations are often identified as "potted," alluding to the jars or crocks they are traditionally stored in. Put up in small servings, these admittedly indulgent treats are completely portable—perfect for picnics and gifting.

DUCK CONFIT

Meat is treated with a dry salt cure before gently poaching in seasoned fat. Cooled and sealed in that same fat, the confit can be held under refrigeration for a very long time. There are as many recipes for duck confit as there are opinionated chefs in the kitchen. The confit is preserved with the salt and fat alone; however, it is traditional to include a mix of some or all of the following spices: cumin, coriander, cinnamon, allspice, black pepper, thyme, bay, cloves, ginger, star anise. Note: Instead of legs and thighs only, you may use an entire duck, cut into pieces; however, white meat is not as rich and will have a different finished texture.

Season: Any time (traditionally, hunting season)
Yield: 6 to 12 servings, depending on final preparation
Store: Refrigerator (6 months), freezer (1 year)

6 large duck legs and thighs, about 5 pounds

3 tablespoons kosher salt

½ teaspoon ground coriander

½ teaspoon ground cinnamon

½ teaspoon ground allspice

½ teaspoon ground ginger

¼ teaspoon freshly ground nutmeg

¼ teaspoon dried thyme

Pinch of ground cloves

1 entire head of garlic, peeled (at least 10 cloves)

2 to 2½ pounds duck fat or a combination of duck fat and lard, rendered (see Rendering Fat on page 132)

Place the duck parts, in a single layer, in a baking dish; sprinkle with the salt, coriander, cinnamon, allspice, ginger, nutmeg, thyme, and cloves, being sure to thoroughly coat the meat on all sides. Cover the dish with plastic wrap and place in the refrigerator to cure for 24 to 36 hours.

Preheat oven to 200°F. Remove the duck from the cure, rinse under cool water, and pat dry with paper towels. Put the duck into an oven-proof pot that will hold it snugly in one or two layers; too large a pot will require more duck or pork fat, as the meat must be completely submerged during the long cooking process.

Place the garlic cloves among the duck parts and pour the liquid fat into the pan to cover. Bring to a simmer over medium high heat. Then place in the oven, uncovered, and cook until the garlic cloves are a rich deep brown, about 6 hours. When done, the very tender meat will settle to the bottom of the dish.

Cool the confit to room temperature, still in its cooking pot. When cool enough to handle, remove the meat and strain the fat into a measuring cup; discard any remaining solids. To pack the meat for long-term storage, pour 1 inch of the strained fat into a scalded storage jar or crock and allow it to harden. Pack the duck on top of the solidified fat to fill the container, allowing at least 1 inch of headspace. Cover completely with the strained fat, ensuring at least a 1-inch layer on top of the meat to seal the container; there should not be any air spaces within the jar.

Cool completely, cover with foil, and store in the refrigerator.

RENDERING FAT

Cut the fat into uniform pieces; place in a heavy saucepan with $\frac{1}{2}$ cup of water over very low heat and cook for several hours to melt. The fat will liquefy and the water will evaporate, leaving the pure rendered fat.

Line a sieve with cheesecloth and strain the fat through into a storage container. The golden-brown cracklings that remain in the cheesecloth may be used to flavor and enrich cornbread, hearty greens, or potato dishes, Cool, cover, and refrigerate or freeze until needed.

Note: Rendered fat may be reused when preparing your next confit, until it becomes too salty.

PORK RILLETTES

· ·

Rillettes are traditionally made with pork shoulder, an inexpensive and somewhat fatty cut of meat. This recipe calls for lean pork loin—a cut that can be somewhat shy on taste—transforming it into a rich, deeply flavored spread. Again, the process is flexible and may include fatty or lean cuts of pork, or poultry legs and thighs, or both. Serve rillettes with crusty bread and cornichon pickles for a light snack or an impressive first course.

> **Season: Any time**
> **Yield: 5 to 6 cups**
> **Store: Refrigerator (6 months), freezer (1 year)**

· ·

3 pounds boneless, fatty pork shoulder or 2½ pounds lean pork
  loin and 1 pound pork fat

1 medium onion, studded with 5 cloves

1 tablespoon kosher salt

1 small bunch fresh thyme or ½ teaspoon dried thyme

½ teaspoon whole allspice

2 bay leaves

½ teaspoon black peppercorns, cracked

Water or white wine or veal stock

Salt and freshly ground pepper

Preheat oven to 275°F.

Cut the pork (and fat if using) into small cubes and combine with the onion, salt, thyme, allspice, bay leaves, and peppercorns in a heavy 6-quart stockpot or Dutch oven. Add water (or a mix of water, wine, and/or stock) to cover and bring to a simmer over medium heat.

Place the pot, covered, in the oven and cook until the meat is tender and falling apart, at least 4 hours. The liquid will have reduced by half and the fat will be completely melted.

Remove the pork to a large bowl to cool; strain the remaining liquid fat and reserve. When the pork is cool enough to handle, pick through it to remove the bay leaves and any apparent whole spices. Using two forks, pull the meat into fine shreds. Alternatively, you can transfer the pork to the bowl of a standing mixer fitted with a paddle attachment and mix on low speed until it is finely shredded.

Taste the pork and season with salt and pepper to taste. Add enough of the reserved liquid fat to create a creamy, spreadable consistency. Pack into individual ramekins or small serving crocks and place in the refrigerator to chill overnight.

The next day, scoop off some of the reserved fat, melt again over low heat, and pour a ¼-inch layer over the top of the cooled rillettes, making sure the fat comes into unbroken contact with the sides of the containers for a complete seal. Return to the refrigerator for at least a couple of days to allow the flavors to ripen.

To serve, scrape off the top layer of fat and serve at room temperature for the fullest flavor. Refrigerate any leftovers and consume within 1 week. For long-term storage, wrap the containers tightly in foil and refrigerate or freeze.

POTTED SHRIMP

This terrine is delicious on crackers, or spread it on thinly sliced rye bread to create elegant tea sandwiches—crusts removed, of course.

Season: Any time
Yield: 2 cups
Store: Refrigerator (2 months)

½ cup (8 tablespoons) unsalted butter, divided
¾ pound cooked tiny shrimp
1 tablespoon freshly squeezed lemon juice
¼ teaspoon cayenne pepper
Salt and freshly ground pepper

Melt 6 tablespoons of the butter over low heat until foamy. Remove from heat; skim off the foam and discard. Mix the shrimp, lemon juice, and cayenne with the melted butter and salt and pepper to taste. Divide the mixture between two 1-cup serving crocks or ramekins. Chill.

Melt the remaining butter and skim the foam as before. Pour the now clarified butter over the chilled shrimp, taking care to leave any sediment in the bottom of the pan. Wrap in plastic and store in the refrigerator.

Variation: For even deeper flavor, start with 1 to 1¼ pounds of larger raw shrimp or prawns in their shells. Poach the shrimp in seasoned water just until pink. Drain and remove the meat from the shells; reserve the shells. Chop the meat finely. Melt 6 tablespoons of the butter over low heat until foamy; skim off the foam. Add the reserved shells to the melted butter. Simmer the shells in the butter for 10 minutes over very low heat; do not allow the butter to brown. Strain the butter to remove the shells and proceed with the main recipe instructions, mixing the shrimp and seasonings together before packing into crocks.

SMOKE IS FLAVOR

Caramelized sugars add depth of color, and complex aromatic compounds imparted by burning wood lend richness and intensity to smoked fish, meat, or cheese. The final effect is highly dependent on the nature of what is burned to produce the smoke; seasoned hardwoods and fruitwoods each offer a unique character. Avoid sappy soft woods and green or treated woods, as they may impart unpleasant or even toxic substances in their smoke.

Small batches of food may be smoked indoors on the stovetop, using a covered roasting pan fitted with a rack and supported by a good exhaust system, or outdoors on a covered grill. More adventuresome cooks or those who have a good deal of fish or meat to process may want to invest in or build an actual box smoker. These methods all create a hot smoking environment, with temperatures between 150 and 200°F, in which food is cooked as well as flavored by smoke. True cold smoking, at temperatures of 100°F and below, cannot be done safely at home without specialized and often expensive equipment.

HOW TO TURN YOUR KETTLE GRILL INTO A SMOKER

Assemble the following supplies:

> Kettle grill with lid
> 2 small, lightweight disposable pans
> Charcoal chimney or electric heating coil for starting coals
> Charcoal briquettes or hardwood lump charcoal
> Smoking wood chips, soaked in water for several hours
> Oven thermometer

Place the pans on the bottom and to one side of the kettle on the lower grill; they should occupy about half of the space at the bottom of the grill. Fill the pans halfway with water. This will provide a moist cooking environment and help to regulate the heat as well as help to prevent flare-ups while the meat is cooking.

Start the coals using either a chimney starter or a heating coil. When the coals are ready (glowing red, with an even coating of gray ash), remove the chimney or coil and arrange the coals to cover the remaining half of the lower grill. Position the cooking grill and place the food to be smoked on it directly over the drip pans. Following the recipe instructions, begin to add soaked wood chips, a few at a time. If your grill has a hinged edge, position it above the coals to facilitate easily adding briquettes during the long cooking process; grills without this hinge must be carefully lifted out of the way as necessary. Cover the grill and close all the vents, top and bottom.

Carefully monitor the grill. There should always be some smoke escaping from under the lid of the kettle. Keep an eye on heat as well; the temperature at grill level should be 225 to 250°F. Heat rises, so if your barbecue has a built-in thermometer on the lid it should read somewhere between 300 and 325°F. For a more accurate reading, place an oven thermometer by the meat. If the temperature gets too high, remove the lid and let the coals burn down a bit; add more soaked wood chips, close the lid, and proceed. If temperature is not hot enough, open the vents to oxygenate the fire. If that doesn't work, add more charcoal. Keep checking the grill every hour or so, adding wood chips and coals as necessary and turning the meat.

SMOKED CHICKEN

. . . .

Brining the bird before smoking keeps the meat moist during its long cooking period; the sugars in the brine create a flavorful, deep-mahogany-colored skin.

Season: Any time
Yield: 1 bird
Store: Refrigerator (1 week), freezer (6 months)

. . . .

1 chicken, 4 to 5 pounds
Water to cover
½ cup kosher salt (per quart of water)
3 tablespoons brown sugar (per quart of water)
½ teaspoon black peppercorns (per quart of water)
½ bay leaf (per quart of water)
Vegetable oil

Rinse the chicken, cleaning the interior cavity well; remove all surplus fat. Put the chicken in a crock or large plastic container and pour in cold water to cover by at least 2 inches. Remove the chicken and refrigerate. Transfer the water into a large saucepan, measuring the amount as you go; this will be your brine. Multiply by the number of quarts and add the resulting amounts of salt, brown sugar, peppercorns, and bay leaf, following the instructions to create a brine (see page 61). Let cool completely.

Put the chicken back in the crock and pour in the fully cooled brine to cover. If necessary, weight it with a plate or other flat, nonmetallic dish to keep it completely submerged. Refrigerate for 18 to 24 hours.

When you are ready to smoke the chicken, heat a grill. Remove the chicken from the brine and rinse it quickly in cool water. Pat the chicken dry with paper towels, taking particular care to dry the inside cavity. Rub all surfaces with a light coating of vegetable oil and truss the chicken as for roasting.

Place the chicken on the prepared grill over the drip pans and slowly roast for 1 hour, then start adding a few soaked smoking chips to the coals. Smoke the chicken until the thickest part of the breast or thigh registers 165 to 170°F on an instant-read meat thermometer, or until the juices run clear. Count on at least 3 hours of cooking time. Monitor the smoke and temperature within the grill, basting the chicken with more vegetable oil if the skin begins to look dry. In general, the rule is "low and slow"; a lower cooking temperature for a longer period of time produces a more succulent result.

Cool the smoked chicken to room temperature for immediate serving, or cool it completely and wrap properly for refrigerator or freezer storage.

Variation: Substitute a turkey breast, bone-in, 5 to 6 pounds, for the chicken.

CHEESE

Welcome to the world of cheese making! It's easier than you think. In the simplest terms, cheese is the result of milk that has been inoculated with an acid, which causes it to coagulate into semisolid curds. The curds are strained out from the remaining liquid, or whey, and drained or pressed to form a solid mass—cheese. Traditionally, cheese was one of the only ways to preserve milk in the absence of refrigeration and when dairy animals didn't produce for as many months of the year as they do today.

Artisanal cheese making is enjoying a popular resurgence in this country, and it is not unusual for even the smallest farmers market to have a least one supplier who produces outstanding cheese. Talk with the cheese maker to learn the seasons and explore the many different varieties of cheese. In the hands of a master, this "simple" process can be the stuff of magic. Every cheese maker has his or her secrets: milk, starter, aging, even the pastures where the animals graze all affect the final product. However, there's another category of cheese that is better suited to average kitchen production methods. The following recipes for fresh cheese, sometimes called "drip" cheeses, involve introducing a controlled coagulant and draining the resulting curds to create a fresh, cream cheese—style spread. These offer us another way to savor and explore the offerings of small dairies producing healthy, fresh milk, cream, and yogurt.

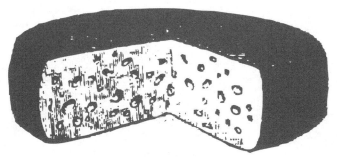

YOGURT CHEESE

Drained overnight, yogurt will lose about 50 percent of its moisture, turning into a rich, tangy, spreadable "cheese." For the best results, start with a whole or low-fat, active-culture yogurt without added gums, stabilizers, or sweeteners; nonfat yogurt produces an overly tart cheese. Try a goat's milk yogurt if you can find it.

Season: Any time
Yield: 1 cup
Store: Refrigerator, 1 week

2 cups whole or low-fat yogurt

Line a sieve or colander with dampened cheesecloth and place it over a bowl. Put the yogurt in a bowl and whisk until smooth, then pour it into the sieve. Refrigerate and let drain for at least 4 hours and up to overnight. Discard the liquid in the catch bowl. Transfer the now-thickened yogurt cheese to a container and refrigerate.

Variations: Herbs, spices, and chopped vegetables may all be added to the finished cheese before serving. Add minced fresh garlic and diced cucumber for a traditional Middle Eastern salad. Dried fruits, honey, and sweet spices may be added for a more dessert-like spread; try this on toasted gingerbread.

FARMER'S CHEESE

* *

Easy to make, this cheese was traditionally made by farmers for home consumption and may be produced from cow's, sheep's, goat's, or more exotic milks.

Season: Any time

Yield: 1 pound

Store: Refrigerator (1 week)

* *

1 gallon whole milk

Large pinch of salt

Freshly squeezed juice of 1 large lemon

Pour the milk into a heavy pot, add the salt, and bring to a simmer over medium heat; stir to prevent the milk from scorching on the bottom of the pot. Turn off the heat when small bubbles appear around the edges. Stir in the lemon juice and allow the milk to sit for 5 to 10 minutes for curds to form.

Line a sieve or colander with dampened cheesecloth and place it over a bowl. Pour in the now-curdled milk to separate the curds from the whey. Discard the whey or reserve it for use in baked goods. When the curds have cooled a bit and the dripping has slowed, draw the four corners of the cheesecloth together, using your hands to form the cheese into a solid mass. Suspend the bagged cheese over a bowl and allow it to drain for at least an hour at cool room temperature (not over 70°F). The longer it drains, the firmer the cheese becomes.

The finished cheese may be flavored with salt, pepper, fresh herbs, spices, and garlic. Keep refrigerated and use within one week.

Variation: Stir a tiny pinch of salt and heavy cream into the finished cheese for a simple dessert. Drizzle with honey and serve with wheatmeal crackers.

QUESO BLANCO

This Latin American cheese is easy to produce at home and has many applications. It has a bland, somewhat sweet flavor and a firm, almost rubbery texture that does not melt. Queso blanco browns nicely, absorbing any flavors it is cooked with; it is often used in recipes to extend meat.

Season: Any time
Yield: 1 pound
Store: Refrigerator (1 week)

1 gallon whole milk
¼ cup cider vinegar
Salt to taste

Pour the milk into a heavy pot and slowly heat to 180°F over very low heat. Stir to prevent the milk from scorching on the bottom of the pot. Remove the pot from heat, stir in the vinegar, and allow the milk to sit while the curds form.

Line a sieve or colander with dampened cheesecloth and place it over a bowl. Pour in the now-curdled milk to separate the curds from the whey. Discard the whey or reserve it for use in baked goods. When the curds have cooled a bit and the dripping has slowed, draw the four corners of the cheesecloth together, using your hands to form the cheese into a solid mass. Suspend the bagged cheese over a bowl and allow it to drain for at least an hour at cool room temperature (not over 70°F). The longer it drains, the firmer the cheese becomes.

Transfer the drained cheese to a bowl and salt to taste. The finished cheese may be used in any recipe that calls for ricotta.

POTTED CHEESE

This is the perfect use for the many bits and pieces of cheese that always seem to accumulate in the cheese drawer; it transforms these leftovers into a savory spread. This recipe is based on a traditional Welsh rabbit, a beer-and-melted-cheese blend. Note: If your leftovers allow, try to balance mild cheeses 3:1 with sharp ones.

Season: Any time
Yield: 2 cups
Store: Refrigerator (6 months)

¾ pound cheese
1 teaspoon dry mustard
⅔ cup good beer
½ cup butter, room temperature
1 teaspoon Worcestershire sauce
Freshly ground pepper
Pinch of cayenne
Salt, if needed
Clarified butter

Grate or chop the cheese into fine bits. Place the cheese and mustard in a bowl, cover with the beer, and stir thoroughly to combine. Cover the bowl and allow the mixture to sit on the counter for a few hours to soften; with hard cheeses it may need to sit out overnight.

Place the butter in the bowl of a food processor and whirl until creamy. Add the beer and cheese mixture, Worcestershire sauce, pepper, and cayenne; process until combined and as smooth as you'd like. Taste for seasoning and make adjustments. The flavor should be assertive.

Pack the finished cheese into one or more serving crocks and smooth the top. Serve at room temperature for the fullest flavor. To store the potted cheese for more than a week, seal the crocks with a ¼ inch layer of melted, clarified butter, taking care to form a good seal all around the edges of the crock. Store in the refrigerator.

Variation: Leave out the dry mustard, Worcestershire sauce, and cayenne, add ½ cup chopped walnuts, and substitute dry sherry for the beer; season to taste with freshly ground nutmeg.

HOW TO MAKE BUTTER

Fresh homemade butter has a clean, pure flavor and is quick and easy to make—a fun job for fidgety kids who can't sit still anyway. Fill a quart jar half full of fresh, heavy cream, cover with a tight-fitting lid, and let it sit at room temperature for 8 to 12 hours or overnight. Shake, roll, or otherwise agitate the jar until the butter begins to separate from the milk and form a separate mass, 20 to 30 minutes.

An easier method, best left to adults, is to whip the heavy cream, using a food processor or blender set on a low speed for 4 to 5 minutes. Keep the sides of the bowl or blender scraped down to produce the greatest yield.

Whichever method you choose, when churning is completed, pour off the remaining liquid through a fine strainer to catch any small particles of butter. Chill this buttermilk for a healthful drink or save it for baking and enriching other dishes. Put the butter into a large bowl of ice water and work it with a wooden spoon or squeeze it gently between your fingers to extract the rest of the buttermilk, which will sour if it is not removed. Refresh the ice water several times and continue to knead the butter until it is smooth and waxy and the water stays clear. Give the butter one final rinse and work in salt if you choose. Pack the finished butter into a crock or shape into a cake and wrap securely in waxed paper. Refrigerate for 48 hours to let the flavor develop before serving.

Quaint, old-fashioned butter churns consisting of a tall, narrow lidded crock and a wooden dasher or plunger may still be found in antique stores. Although still perfectly functional, they are somewhat impractical unless you have a great deal of cream to process.

Certain volatile solids in butter are apt to become rancid in warm climates. Long, slow heating separates these milk solids from the remaining fat; the flavor is altered, but what remains is shelf stable, even at very warm temperatures. This clarified butter or ghee is a staple cooking oil in many hot climates where butter quickly spoils.

ETHIOPIAN SPICED GHEE

This delicious condiment is highly seasoned and completely shelf stable when covered to keep out moisture and light.

Season: Any time
Yield: About 2 cups
Store: Refrigerator (6 months)

2 cups unsalted butter
4 tablespoons chopped onion
1 ½ tablespoons chopped garlic
2 tablespoons grated fresh ginger
½ teaspoon turmeric
2 whole cardamom pods, crushed (or ½ teaspoon
    ground cardamom)
1 cinnamon stick, 2 to 3 inches
2 or 3 whole cloves
⅛ teaspoon freshly grated nutmeg

Melt the butter and bring it to a boil in a heavy pan over medium heat. When the butter begins to foam, add the remaining ingredients and simmer for one hour without stirring. The solids will separate out and sink to the bottom of the pan; do not allow the solids to brown. Carefully strain the clear liquid through a fine sieve lined with dampened cheesecloth, leaving the solids in the bottom of the pan. Strain the liquid two more times. Pour the strained, clarified spiced ghee into a scalded jar and cover.

EGGS

More eggs are laid during the months of March, April, May, and June than in all the other months combined. Properly treated, freshly laid eggs will keep for about 6 weeks under cool, moist conditions; if you are using a self-defrosting refrigerator, seal the eggs in a plastic container to maintain a higher level of humidity. Do not wash eggs you intend to store in the shell. Washing removes a gelatinous protective coating that seals out bacteria and helps prevent evaporation. Simply wipe with a soft cloth to remove dirt, then store, small end down. Nonfertile eggs—from hens without access to roosters—will keep longer than fertile eggs.

Whether you keep laying hens yourself, are lucky enough to know someone who does, or simply purchase exquisitely fresh eggs at the farmers market, pickling eggs helps preserve the bounty and adds mealtime variety to those egg-centric months of the calendar.

PICKLED EGGS

A standard menu item in British pubs and taverns, pickled eggs are a delicious and economical way to preserve eggs for several months under refrigeration. This recipe and the two that follow are perfect for picnics and make a beautiful presentation for cocktail snacks. Note: Small or medium eggs, sometimes called "pullets," cure the quickest.

Season: Any time
Yield: 2 dozen eggs, about 2 quarts
Store: Refrigerator (3 months)

3 cups distilled white vinegar

1 cup water

1 small onion or 2 to 3 shallots, peeled and thinly sliced

2 teaspoons kosher salt

1 tablespoon sugar

2 tablespoons pickling spices (page 102)

2 dozen eggs, hardboiled, cooled, and peeled

Bring the vinegar, water, onion, salt, sugar, and spices to a boil over medium heat; simmer, covered, for 3 minutes.

Place the eggs in 1 large or 2 quart-sized scalded jars. Pour the hot brine over the eggs, dividing the spice mixture evenly between the two jars. The eggs should be completely submerged in liquid; if not, top up with more vinegar. Cool to room temperature, seal the jar(s), and refrigerate for a week or two before serving.

Variation: Cinnamon, cloves, fresh ginger, and garlic may individually or in combination be added to the above recipe for added flavor. Adding 1 teaspoon of ground turmeric will produce deep-golden-colored finished eggs.

ALL-AMERICAN RED BEET EGGS

These eggs, quickly pickled with spiced beets and onions, are a popular tradition among the Pennsylvania Dutch.

Season: Any time

Yield: About 2 quarts

Store: Refrigerator (3 months)

1 dozen eggs, hardboiled, cooled, and peeled

2 cups canned or freshly cooked peeled beets in their cooking liquid

1 small onion, peeled and thinly sliced

1 cup cider vinegar

½ cup sugar

1 teaspoon kosher salt

Drain the beets, reserving the liquid. Put the eggs, beets, and onion in 1 large scalded jar or divide between 2 quart-sized scalded jars.

Combine the beet liquid, vinegar, sugar, and salt in a small saucepan, bring to a boil, and simmer for 5 minutes, stirring to dissolve the sugar completely.

Pour the hot brine over the contents of the jar(s) to cover. Cool to room temperature, seal the jar(s), and refrigerate for at least 1 week before serving.

CHINESE MARBLED TEA EGGS

In the absence of a brine or vinegar, these eggs—cooked with strong black tea and seasoned with orange peel and Asian spices—should be eaten within a few days of preparing.

Season: Any time
Yield: 1 dozen eggs
Store: Refrigerator (1 week)

1 dozen eggs, room temperature

3 tablespoons kosher salt

2 tablespoons Chinese five-spice powder

1 star anise

6 tea bags or 3 tablespoons loose, black tea

2 tablespoons soy sauce

One 2-inch strip of tangerine zest, bitter white pith removed

Cover the eggs with water and bring to a boil for 3 to 5 minutes. Drain and cool.

When cool enough to handle, gently tap each egg with the back of a spoon to evenly crack the shell all over; do NOT remove the shell.

Place the eggs back in the saucepan, add the salt, spice, star anise, tea, soy sauce, and zest and add water to just cover the eggs. Return to the heat and simmer for 1 hour. Drain the eggs and remove the shells to reveal the beautiful marbled surface. The finished eggs may be served warm or cold, sliced in quarters.

Variation: Add 3 tablespoons sugar for a sweeter version; cool overnight in the tea mixture for a stronger flavor.

HERBS AND FLOWERS

E ven the smallest urban patio, windowsill, or stoop usually has room for a satisfying pot of herbs, whose lively flavors can be savored fresh throughout the growing season. The following recipes help carry your herbal harvest beyond the close of summer. Premixed blends of home-dried herbs are an easy timesaver; packaged nicely, they make a lovely gift.

HERB BOUQUETS

The bouquet garni (French for "garnished bouquet") consists of a small bunch of herbs tied together with string and cooked or steeped with soups, stews, and sauces. Bundling the herbs allows the cook to easily remove them before the dish is served, for a refined presentation. Herb bouquets may be used fresh or dried and packaged for future use.

For each bouquet start with a bay leaf and a small bundle of thyme.

▶ For beef, add marjoram, savory, and a *small* sprig of rosemary

▶ For fish, add dried fennel or fennel seed and celery leaves

▶ For poultry, add tarragon and a *small* sprig of lemon thyme

▶ For pork, good additions are sage, fennel, marjoram, and rosemary

▶ For tomato sauces, add basil and oregano

HERBES DE PROVENCE

. . . .

This traditional blend of herbs native to the sunny climes of southern France is delicious with goat cheese or sprinkled on vegetables or chicken before roasting.

. . . .

Combine equal parts of basil, thyme, summer savory, marjoram, and rosemary with one-half part lavender and a twist of dried orange zest.

CHINESE FIVE-SPICE BLEND

. . . .

A flavorful and spicy blend for Asian dishes, this is also good dusted on sliced oranges for an interesting side dish.

. . . .

> 2 tablespoons black peppercorns
> 40 whole cloves
> 3 cinnamon sticks, 2 to 3 inches long
> 2 tablespoons fennel seed
> 12 whole star anise

Whirl all the ingredients in a blender or clean coffee grinder, processing to a fine powder. Store in an airtight container.

HERBS IN OIL

The essence and flavor of many herbs, spices, and aromatic vegetables can be extracted and preserved to create a savory condiment that sings of the garden. Infused oils add hearty character to salad dressings or a quick sauté or when brushed on grilled meats and vegetables. Although every bit as versatile in the kitchen as herbal vinegars, flavored oils are more subject to spoiling. To enjoy these delicious creations at their best, put up smaller quantities, share with friends, and use generously. In warm climates, store infused oils in the refrigerator to extend their shelf life.

You can infuse a single herb or build more complex flavors with a blend of herbs and spices. A mild peanut or vegetable oil allows the herb flavor to dominate the finished infusion; extra-virgin olive oil, which may overpower some herbs, complements strong flavors like garlic and chilies.

Put 1 cup of herbs and flavorings into a clean, dry 1-quart jar and fill with oil; steep for at least 2 weeks. Make sure all the ingredients are completely submerged in oil; if any are exposed, mold will develop. When the flavor is to your liking, strain the oil into bottles, cap or cork, and store away from heat. A decorative sprig of an identifying herb may be added to the finished bottle.

PROVENÇAL OIL

· ·

This heady blend is redolent of the Mediterranean and lends a rich flavor to the simplest preparations—just heating this oil in a pan for a quick sauté perfumes the kitchen with mouth-watering aromas.

Season: Mid- to late summer

Yield: 1 quart

Store: Cool, dark pantry (3 months)

· ·

One 6-inch branch of fresh rosemary

Several sprigs fresh thyme

3 bay leaves

2 cloves garlic, peeled and split

1 teaspoon black peppercorns

Several strips fresh orange zest, bitter white pith removed

3 stems lavender blossoms, fresh or dried

1 small sprig fresh oregano

1 tablespoon fennel seed, toasted

Olive oil

Make sure all the herbs are clean and perfectly dry. Put the ingredients into a scrupulously clean quart bottle; a clean chopstick is effective for arranging everything in a pleasing manner. Using a funnel, fill the bottle with olive oil to completely cover the herbs.

Cork the bottle securely and place in a cool place for one month to allow the flavors to permeate the oil. Impatient cooks can place the corked bottle on a windowsill where the gentle heat of the sun will speed up the extraction process. As the oil is used, top up the bottle with more oil or decant into a smaller bottle so that the herbs are not above the level of the oil in the upright bottle, which would cause them to spoil. In warm climates, the finished oil should be stored in the refrigerator; chilling will cloud the oil, but the flavor will be unaffected and the oil will clear upon returning to room temperature.

HOT CHILI ORANGE OIL

This bright orange, deeply flavored oil builds to a slow burn. It is delicious on cold noodle salads, with peanut chicken or tofu, and mixed with soy sauce for dipping spring rolls and dim sum.

Season: Any time
Yield: 2 ½ cups
Store: Cool, dark pantry (6 months)

3 large organic oranges
½ cup dried hot red chili flakes
3 cloves garlic, peeled and lightly smashed
1 tablespoon fermented black bean paste
2 cups peanut or canola oil

Scrub the oranges with a soft brush and mild soap to remove any vegetable wax. With a sharp vegetable peeler or paring knife, remove the bright orange zest from the fruit in large strips, avoiding the bitter white pith. Finely mince the zest.

Combine the zest with the chili flakes, garlic, bean paste, and oil in a heavy 2-quart saucepan. Bring to a low boil over medium heat and simmer for 15 minutes. Caution: the chili fumes coming off the simmering oil are powerful; avoid direct contact with eyes or nose! Remove from heat and let stand until cool.

Store the oil with its seasonings in a glass jar, covered, at room temperature.

HERBAL COMPOUND BUTTER

A classic element of haute cuisine. Make an assortment of blends and store them in the freezer for a quick finishing touch for grilled meats, pasta, and vegetables.

Season: Summer through fall
Yield: ½ **pound**
Store: Freezer (6 months)

1 cup butter, preferably unsalted

5 tablespoons finely chopped fresh herbs, or herb and edible flower blend, or 2½ teaspoons herb seed, pulverized

1 teaspoon freshly squeezed lemon juice

Salt and freshly ground pepper

Lemon zest (optional)

Cream the butter in a standing mixer or by hand until very light and fluffy. Add the herbs, lemon juice, salt, pepper, and zest and blend well. Pack the finished butter into a crock or shape into a cylinder and wrap tightly in waxed paper; the roll can be sliced for serving. Store finished butters in the freezer.

The number of possible flavor combinations is limited only by your imagination and access to fresh herbs. Butter is a perfect medium to store herbs and retain their bright garden flavors.

Possible blends and serving suggestions:

- Mint and chive—spring lamb, potatoes, peas
- Fennel seed and tarragon or chervil—fish, egg dishes
- Rose geranium, lavender, and honey—toast, scones
- Parsley, chives, and marjoram—all-purpose, good on grilled meats
- Dill and mustard seed—snap beans, potatoes, white fish
- Garlic, parsley, and oregano—hot bread, pasta, vegetables
- Ginger, orange zest, and thyme—pork, chicken, rice, carrots
- Thyme, savory, and black pepper—snap beans, chicken

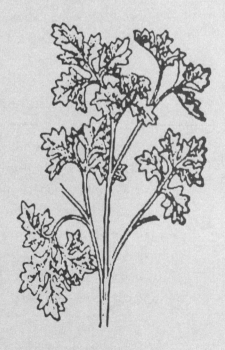

PESTO

Basil is what we think of most often when pesto is mentioned. A fine paste of olive oil, fresh basil, pine nuts, and garlic, finished with parmesan cheese, basil pesto is delicious on pasta, grilled chicken, tomato salads, or simply crusty bread—a definite highlight of the summer herb season. Carry this flavor into the colder months of the year by freezing pesto in small, serving-size quantities—an ice cube tray is perfect for this—and packaging in zip-locking freezer bags.

Season: Late summer through fall
Yield: About 2 cups
Store: Refrigerator or freezer (6 months)

3 to 3½ cups fresh green basil, firmly packed
¾ to 1 cup good olive oil
3 cloves garlic, peeled
¼ cup pine nuts
Salt
Parmesan cheese (omit if freezing)

Purée the basil, olive oil, garlic, and pine nuts in a blender or bowl of a food processor to the degree of coarseness you prefer. Scrape the purée into a bowl and add salt to taste. Stir in several handfuls of parmesan cheese and serve. To store in the refrigerator, pack the pesto into a jar and top with a layer of olive oil to keep the paste from darkening from exposure to the air. To freeze, omit the parmesan cheese and pack the container, leaving ½ inch headspace, or fill ice cube trays as suggested; add cheese when serving.

Variation: Substitute mint, cilantro, tarragon, or parsley for all or part of the basil; substitute coarsely chopped toasted walnuts for the pine nuts.

HERBAL VINEGARS

The ephemeral flavor of some herbs simply is not fully captured by drying or freezing. Creating herb vinegars is one way to preserve the delicacy of tarragon, chervil, borage, and salad burnet. Select a neutral white wine vinegar or the slightly sweet, but very mild rice wine vinegar to allow the herbal flavors to come through cleanly. Other, more assertive herbs—like basil, rosemary, oregano, and thyme—will hold up in stronger cider or red wine vinegar infusions.

The general ratio is 1 cup fresh herb to 1 quart vinegar. Combine herb(s) and vinegar in a glass jar with a nonreactive lid and place on a sunny windowsill to steep for 2 weeks where the heat of the sun will work to extract the herb's flavor. Strain the vinegar and taste. For a stronger flavor, repeat this procedure with another batch of fresh herbs and steep for another 2 weeks. Strain and bottle.

For a quicker result—or in less sunny months of the year—bring vinegar just to the boiling point. Place the herbs in a glass container and fill with the hot vinegar. Let steep until cool and strain into decorative bottles.

Suggested herbs:

- Chives and chive blossoms add a hint of mild onion flavor and a beautiful blush pink color.
- Dill is great in fish and potato dishes; add a seed head to the finished bottle for a decorative touch.
- Borage blossoms impart a slight blue tint to the finished vinegar; add chopped leaves and stems for a strong cucumber flavor.
- Mint vinegar makes a good marinade for lamb and adds spark to fruit salads.
- Chervil, fennel, and tarragon all have a delicate anise flavor, best captured in a mild vinegar.

▶ Basil complements tomato, pasta salads, and other vegetables;
red basil makes a beautiful ruby-colored vinegar.

▶ Lavender, violet, scented geranium, and other floral vinegars
provide zest to fruit salads and other sweet dishes.

AND MORE

Although we commonly think of herbs primarily in relation to savory
dishes, they also complement many sweet treatments. Think herb jelly
on buttered toast, lavender honey in hot tea, candied violets on cakes,
cookies sprinkled with herb sugar—even infused herbal syrups as a base
for exciting cocktails and refreshing drinks. Where sweet and savory
meet in the middle, herbs enhance and heighten flavors.
Rosemary jelly or herbal honey served with sharp
cheese makes a delicious appetizer or after-dinner
cheese course.

BASIC HERB JELLY

Fresh apple juice provides an almost neutral flavor base and plenty of natural pectin to produce beautiful, clear herb jelly.

Season: Summer through fall
Yield: 2 to 3 pints
Store: Cool, dark pantry

6 pounds apples, coarsely chopped, including skins and cores
Fresh herbs (suggestions follow)
Sugar
2 to 3 tablespoons lemon juice

Put the chopped apples in a heavy preserving pan, barely cover with water, and simmer for 30 minutes or until very soft. Transfer the mixture to a jelly bag or a colander lined with dampened cheesecloth; drain overnight, collecting the juices in a bowl.

Combine the apple juice and fresh herbs and bring to a boil; cover the pan, remove from heat, and steep until the liquid is completely cooled. Strain and measure the herb-infused juice into the preserving pan, adding 1 cup of sugar for every cup of juice. Taste and add lemon juice to achieve a pleasing tartness. Bring to a boil, stirring constantly, and cook until the mixture reaches 220°F on a kitchen thermometer or otherwise passes the jelly-doneness test (see page 76). Remove from heat.

Carefully ladle the hot jelly into hot, sterilized pint or half-pint jars, allowing ¼ inch headspace; a sprig of fresh herb may be added to each jar for decoration. Follow water-bath canning instructions (page 34) and process for 10 minutes.

Variation: Fresh apple juice or cider may be substituted for the apples; begin the process with steeping the herbs.

Suggested herb jellies:

▶ Scented geranium

▶ Lavender

▶ Mint (a drop or two of green food color will improve the drab green color of natural mint jelly and still fall far short of the lurid commercial product)

▶ Basil, lemon basil, red basil

▶ Rosemary

▶ Sage

▶ Thyme

▶ Rose (remove the bitter white heel from each petal before steeping)

QUICK HERB JELLY

. . . .

This recipe relies on liquid pectin, allowing water, fruit juice, or wine to serve as the infused liquid for an even greater flavor variety.

Season: Summer through fall
Yield: 2 ½ pints
Store: Cool, dark pantry

. . . .

2 cups water or 2½ cups fruit juice or wine

1 cup fresh herbs, chopped

4 cups sugar

¼ cup cider vinegar or lemon juice

3 ounces liquid pectin

Put the herbs in a heat-proof bowl. Bring the liquid to a boil over medium heat and pour it over the herbs. Allow to steep until completely cooled. Strain the finished infusion.

Combine 2 cups of the herbal infusion with the sugar and vinegar or lemon juice. Bring to a boil, stirring to dissolve the sugar completely. Add the pectin and stir the boiling mixture for exactly one minute. Remove the jelly from the heat and skim off any foam.

Carefully ladle the hot jelly into hot, sterilized pint or half-pint jars, allowing ¼ inch headspace; a sprig of fresh herb may be added to each jar for decoration. Follow water-bath canning instructions (page 34) and process for 10 minutes.

Other fruit juice or wine and herb combinations:

- ▶ Orange juice with rosemary, thyme, lavender, or basil
- ▶ Grapefruit juice with tarragon, mint, or marjoram
- ▶ White wine with lemon geranium, dill, tarragon, rose petals, or lemon thyme
- ▶ Red wine with garlic, rosemary, thyme, or oregano

HERBAL TEAS AND BEVERAGES

Many herbs from the garden, fresh or dried, can be steeped in boiling water for a refreshing tea; technically speaking, unless the mixture actually contains true tea, these infusions are called "tisanes." Whatever you call them, depending on what you select, herbal teas can offer a bracing good morning, an afternoon pick-me-up, or a soothing nightcap. Experiment, choosing just one herb for a single-note tea, or mixing several to create your own house blend.

Dry each herb individually before blending, and store tea in airtight containers out of direct light. To brew, combine 1 to 2 teaspoons of tea with 1 cup boiling water; steep for 5 to 8 minutes and strain. Serve with hot milk and sweeten to taste with sugar or honey.

Suggested combinations:

- 4 parts dried lemon verbena and 1 part lavender flowers (a little lavender goes a long way)
- Equal parts peppermint, lemon balm, and fennel seed (good for calming stomach upset)
- 3 parts chamomile flowers and lemon balm, 2 parts catnip, 1 part mint (nighty-night)
- Equal parts lemon balm and spearmint with orange zest and whole cloves
- Basil, fennel, and mints all make a great after-dinner tea (eases indigestion)
- Black or green tea with dried rose petals

SAGE TEA

* * *

A very "green" tasting tea with a lemony zing. Sage has many healthful properties; this tea will effectively soothe a sore throat.

Season: Mid- to late summer

Yield: 4 cups

Store: Serve immediately

* * *

½ cup fresh sage leaves, lightly torn

Sugar or honey, to taste

2 strips lemon zest

Freshly squeezed juice of 1 lemon

4 cups water

Bring the water to a boil and add the remaining ingredients. Cover and steep for 30 minutes. Strain and serve hot or over ice.

GINGER SYRUP

· ·

The gentle heat of fresh ginger is enlivened with citrus for a refreshing homemade ginger ale. Mix the syrup with boiling water for a warming winter toddy.

Season: Any time
Yield: 2 cups
Store: Refrigerator (1 month)

· ·

1½ cups sliced fresh ginger, peeled
1½ cups water
1½ cups sugar
½ cup fresh lemon or lime juice

Combine the ginger, water, and sugar in a heavy saucepan and bring to a boil over medium heat, stirring to dissolve the sugar completely. Simmer for 15 minutes. Remove from the heat, strain, and cool to room temperature. Stir in lemon or lime juice. Bottle and store in the refrigerator. The remaining now-candied ginger slices may be chopped up and added to baked goods or other dishes that would benefit from their sweet, hot flavor; store in the refrigerator for up to 1 month.

To serve, in a tall glass filled with ice, combine 2 tablespoons syrup with sparkling water to taste. Stir gently and garnish with a wedge of lemon or lime.

Variation: For an extra spicy hit, add 2 cardamom pods, crushed, 4 whole cloves, and ½ teaspoon black peppercorns to the simmering ginger syrup.

FRESH GINGER IN SHERRY

. . . .

This recipe not only preserves fresh ginger for use in cooking but also produces a flavorful sherry—an unusual addition to sauces and soups or an interesting twist on a before-dinner aperitif.

> **Season: Any time**
> **Yield: Variable**
> **Store: Cool, dark pantry or refrigerator**

. . . .

> Fresh ginger, peeled and cut into ⅛-inch "coins"
> Dry sherry

Put the ginger in a hot sterilized jar and, using a funnel, add sherry to cover completely. Cork or cap and allow to age for 1 month to infuse the sherry; the ginger may be used at any time.

HOT PEPPERS IN VODKA

The length of steeping time determines the final level of spiciness—it doesn't take long. The perfect foundation for a zesty Bloody Mary cocktail.

Season: Late summer into fall
Yield: 1 pint
Store: Cool, dark pantry or freezer

2 cups good-quality vodka

2 fresh cayenne or other hot red peppers, halved

2 tablespoons black peppercorns

¼ teaspoon imported paprika or pure ground chilies

Combine all the ingredients in a clean dry jar and let stand for 1 to 2 days out of direct sun and away from heat. Taste after 1 day to see how strong the peppers are and determine how hot you want your finished infusion to be.

When the flavor is to your liking, strain into a pitcher or measuring cup; let stand, covered, overnight to allow any sediment to settle. Decant the finished vodka into a clean bottle, leaving the sediment behind. Cap or cork and store in the freezer for serving.

Variation: Gin may be substituted for the vodka.

HERB SYRUP

Preserve the fresh flavor of herbs in sweet sugar syrup that you can use to sweeten iced or hot tea, mix with sparkling water for an all natural herbal soda, or add to lemonade or other juices to create refreshing summer coolers and cocktails.

Season: Summer through fall
Yield: About 1½ cups
Store: Refrigerator (3 months)

3 cups water
1 cup fresh herbs
2 cups sugar

Bring the water to a boil in a saucepan over medium heat. Remove from heat and add the herbs; cover and steep for several hours to make a strong infusion. Strain the liquid into a nonreactive pan, add the sugar, and bring to a boil, stirring to dissolve the sugar completely. Boil without stirring to thicken, about 10 to 12 minutes. Remove from heat, cool, and bottle. The syrup keeps well in the refrigerator.

LAVENDER LEMONADE COOLER

You can substitute thyme, mint, pineapple sage, or rosemary syrup for the lavender syrup. Mix things up at your next summer cocktail party by offering a variety of herbal syrups together with the rest of the makings for this refreshing cooler.

Season: Mid- to late summer
Yield: Variable
Store: Serve immediately

Lavender syrup (see opposite)
Freshly squeezed lemon juice
Vodka
Sparkling wine, chilled
Fresh blueberries and raspberries
Sliced lemons
1 stem fresh lavender

Combine the lavender syrup with the lemon juice for a sweet/tart base. Fill tall glasses with ice; add 1 shot of vodka to each glass. Add the lavender-lemon syrup to three-quarters full. Garnish with berries, a lemon slice, and a lavender sprig and top up with sparkling wine.

Variation: For an alcohol-free version, combine herbal syrup, lemon juice, and sparkling water to taste; add garnish.

HERBAL SUGARS

. . . .

Simple white granulated sugar will absorb the flavorful oils from herbs and other seasonings to create a nuanced sweetener for hot tea, buttered toast, pastry, cakes, and cookies. This quick and easy project makes a lovely gift.

Season: Spring through fall
Yield: ½ pint
Store: Cool, dark pantry (1 year)

. . . .

1 cup sugar
Fresh herbs like lavender, scented geranium leaves, rose petals,
    violets, lemon balm, bay leaf

Select herbs and flowers at their peak of fragrance; make sure they are clean of dust and grit. Remove any bitter white heel from the flower petals; snip stems short or separate into individual leaves. Lay the herbs out on a wire cooling rack to dry overnight and concentrate their oils.

Into a ½ pint jar, layer the herbs and flowers with the sugar until the jar is filled. Cap and store for a couple of weeks for the sugar to absorb the flavor. The finished sugar may be sifted or the herbs and flowers may remain in the sugar to identify the flavor.

Variation: Layer sugar with a supple vanilla bean, cut in half lengthwise and split open.

LAVENDER HONEY

. . . .

Not only is this honey exquisite in tea or on toast and cheese but, due to the antibacterial properties of both the lavender and the honey, this sweet concoction also makes a soothing balm for minor scrapes and inflammations.

Season: Summer
Yield: ½ pint
Store: Room temperature (6 months)

. . . .

6 to 8 lavender stems, blossoms partially open

Harvest the lavender just before the blossoms fully open. Roll them gently in a dry paper towel to remove any garden dust. Cut the stems to fit and put them in a glass jar. Heat 1 cup of honey in the microwave or on the stovetop until quite warm and liquefied. Pour the warm honey into the jar over the lavender buds and seal the jar tightly. Allow to steep for several days; the lavender oil will infuse the honey with a deliciously floral scent and flavor.

Variations: Rose petal, sage blossom, rosemary, sweet bay, pine.

SUGARED VIOLETS

Use these sparkling sugar confections to decorate cakes, puddings, and other springtime desserts.

Season: Spring
Yield: Variable
Store: Cool, dark pantry (6 months)

Sweet violet flowers (*Viola odorata*)
1 egg white
Superfine sugar

Carefully dust each blossom for grit and remove the stems; the flowers must be perfectly dry. In a small bowl, whisk the egg white with 1 teaspoon of water until slightly thinned. Dip a small brush in the egg white and lightly coat each flower. Sprinkle with superfine sugar to thoroughly cover and place on a sheet of parchment or waxed paper in a warm room to dry completely, 24 to 36 hours, depending on atmospheric humidity. Store the candied flowers in an airtight container out of direct light.

Variation: Borage blossoms, individual lilac florets, pansy petals, and rose petals may all be candied; remove the bitter white heel from the base of each rose petal before sugaring.

BEST PRESERVING METHODS

Food	Freeze	Can	Dry	Live Storage	Jam/Jelly Sauce	Vinegar	Alcohol	Salt, Fat, Smoke
Apples	X	X	X	X	X			
Apricots	X	X	X		X		X	
Berries (most)	X	X			X	X	X	
Cherries	X	X	X		X	X	X	
Cranberries	X	X	X		X	X	X	
Figs	X	X	X		X			
Peaches	X	X	X		X	X	X	
Pears	X	X	X	X	X	X	X	
Plums	X	X	X		X	X	X	
Rhubarb	X	X			X			
Strawberries	X				X	X	X	
Tomatoes	X	X	X	X	X			X
Artichokes	X			X		X		
Beans, shell			X					
Beans, snap	X	X				X		X
Beets	X	X		X		X		
Broccoli	X							
Brussels sprouts	X	X						
Cabbage				X		X		X
Carrots	X	X		X		X		
Corn	X	X	X					

Food	Freeze	Can	Dry	Live Storage	Jam/Jelly Sauce	Vinegar	Alcohol	Salt, Fat, Smoke
Cucumbers						X		X
Eggplants		X				X		
Endive				X				
Greens	X							
Herbs (differs by type)	X		X		X	X	X	X
Kale				X				
Leeks	X			X				
Mushrooms	X		X			X		
Okra	X	X				X		
Onions	X		X	X		X		
Parsnips				X				
Peas	X	X	X					
Peppers, hot	X	X	X			X	X	X
Peppers, sweet	X	X				X		X
Potatoes				X				
Pumpkins	X	X		X				
Rutabagas, turnips				X				
Squash, summer	X					X		
Squash, winter	X	X		X				

Food	Freeze	Can	Dry	Live Storage	Jam/Jelly Sauce	Vinegar	Alcohol	Salt, Fat, Smoke
Beef	x		x					x
Chicken	x							x
Fish	x	x	x					x
Game	x							x
Pork	x		x					x
Milk	x					x		x
Butter	x							x
Eggs	x			x		x		

SEASONAL RECIPE GUIDE

CARLA'S LEGACY

Carla Emery grew up on a sheep ranch in Montana and was educated at Columbia University. In the early 1970s she settled on a farm in northern Idaho, where she wrote the first edition of *The Encyclopedia of Country Living*. Originally entitled *Carla Emery's Old Fashioned Recipe Book* and produced on a mimeograph machine in her living room, the book launched its author to the forefront of the back-to-the-land movement.

Growing Your Own Vegetables is the first in a series of single-subject guides drawn from material that appears in *The Encyclopedia of Country Living*, now in its tenth edition. I'm pleased, proud, and delighted to have been asked to author these works for many reasons—not the least of which is my growing fascination with writing about gardening and food, but also because—as my editor put it—I "understand the ethos" of what Carla set out to accomplish when she began so many years ago.

In Seattle during the 1960s and '70s, while Carla was girding herself for society's collapse, I was riding my Sting-Ray bike, hula-hooping, and bopping to AM radio, blissfully oblivious about the world's superpowers flexing their nuclear muscles. After college, in a somewhat belated "flower child" period marked by a fierce streak of independence,

I purchased one of Carla's earliest editions. I was determined to bake our bread and grow our food. However, life in the city is forgiving—if something went awry or I got tired, we simply went out to eat! This was hardly the stuff of self-sufficiency, but still reflective of my desire to be a part of the process and an early awareness of a food web growing increasingly industrial and removed from daily life.

Thankfully, at present, the pendulum is swinging the other way. Increasingly our eyes are open to where our food comes from and how it is produced. More and more, clean, healthy food; safe, sustainable growing practices; and fair living conditions are attracting mainstream concern.

Carla Emery remained a tireless advocate of self-sufficiency and environmental stewardship until her death in 2005. Today's "green living" movement owes a tremendous debt of gratitude to Carla and others like her, who never gave up their pursuit of a good and healthy existence. These contemporary pioneers resuscitated and breathed new life into the skills and traditions of our grandparents and their parents. We may not have more than a tiny patch in the backyard or a few containers on a shyly proportioned patio, but there is still plenty we can grow . . . and plenty more we can learn in the process.

Lorene Edwards Forkner—freelance writer, garden designer, and food enthusiast—revels in the seasonal pleasures and broad scope of gardening in the Pacific Northwest. She is currently at work on additional titles drawn from material found in The Encyclopedia of Country Living. *Follow her work by visiting her Web site, PlantedatHome.com.*

ACKNOWLEDGMENTS

Thank you, Sasquatch Books. Books and by definition publishers, editors, authors, and the many other voices it takes to produce them—open our eyes to possibilities and empower our thinking. The good ones can even change our lives. In this age of digital media and online "content," black ink and paper pages are a labor of love and a sustained commitment. I am especially grateful to Gary Luke, my editor at Sasquatch, for inviting me along on this continuing adventure.

The clarion voices of impassioned writers (and eaters) have opened our eyes to the possibilities each of us has to actively participate in the seasons and reconnect with a healthy food system. Many, many thanks to MaryJane Butters and her warm, embracing, incredibly hardworking family and crew who graciously welcomed me for a farm visit and a magical sleepover under the stars. In many ways similar to Carla Emery, theirs is the voice of can-do resourcefulness and community as they foster a contemporary twenty-first century "farm girl" mentality.

The supportive enthusiasm and enormous heart of my long-time friend Debra Prinzing continuously provides me with the inspiration, motivation, and courage to find my written voice and declare it.

As I learn the writing ropes from this seasoned professional, I am being tutored in the even more lasting language of friendship.

My work would not be possible were it not for the rock-solid support and encouragement of James Forkner, my husband and enduring partner in our household's oftentimes scary but satisfying self-employment economic model. This year's rewards line our pantry's shelves and enhance our feasts with friends and family. My children Hilary and Max are nearly grown, and perhaps my most successful batch yet. "I love you more than roses," please won't you help me pick berries next summer?

—LEF

BIBLIOGRAPHY

Carcy, Nora, *Perfect Preserves*. New York: Stewart, Tabori, & Chang, 1990

Costenbader, Carol, *The Big Book of Preserving the Harvest*. Pownal, VT: Storey Publishing, 1997

Costner, Susan, *Gifts of Food*. New York: Crown Publishers, Inc., 1984

Emery, Carla, *The Encyclopedia of Country Living*, 10th edition. Seattle, WA: Sasquatch Books, 2008

Rombauer, Irma and Marion Rombauer Becker, *Joy of Cooking*. New York: Bobbs-Merrill Company, 1975

Ruhlman, Michael and Brian Polcyn, *Charcuterie: The Craft of Salting, Smoking, and Curing*. New York: W. W. Norton & Company, Inc., 2005

Tolley, Emelie and Chris Mead, *The Herbal Pantry*. New York: Clarkson Potter, 1992

Witty, Helen, *Fancy Pantry*. New York: Workman Publishing, 1986

Witty, Helen and Elizabeth Schneider Colchie, *Better Than Storebought*. New York: Harper & Row Publishing, 1979

INDEX